SPARKLING
WINE for Modern Times

SPARKLING WINE for Modern Times

A DRINKER'S GUIDE TO THE FREEWHEELING WORLD OF BUBBLES

Zachary Sussman

Illustrations by Nick Hensley

PUNCH

TEN SPEED PRESS
California | New York

CONTENTS

Introduction

We've all encountered that guy at the dinner party who makes a big show of correcting you for calling the sparkling wine in your glass "Champagne" even though it comes from somewhere outside the celebrated region of France.

In 2017, however, Canadian Daniel MacDuff took this standard wine-snob microaggression to an extreme when he filed for damages against Sunwing Airlines, a Toronto-based budget carrier, for serving passengers a generic sparkling wine in place of the advertised "complimentary onboard champagne toast." Given the nature of the offense, a class-action lawsuit definitely seems excessive. (The airline dismissed MacDuff's case as "frivolous and without merit.") Nevertheless, there's a lesson to be gleaned from the incident.

Typically, when someone "winesplains" that common talking point about Champagne's delimited zone of production, the implication is that, in the words of the 1968 Marvin Gaye and Tammi Terrell hit, "There ain't nothing like the real thing"—the real thing, of course, being the French original. Across the ages, the region didn't just define the sparkling wine paradigm, it *was* the paradigm; synonymous with all things bubbly.

So you could forgive Sunwing for using the *C* word to delineate the entire category. People have been making the same mistake forever. But if Champagne once represented the sole archetype for fizzy wine, all it takes is a quick survey of today's diverse sparkling landscape to reveal how that old formulation has cracked apart. We've finally bid adieu to the dark ages of the not-so-distant past, when the world of sparkling wine conformed to a simple binary: on the one hand was Champagne, and on the other was pretty much everything else.

Within the span of a decade, all the old rules of engagement have been discarded and written anew. Not only are we drinking our fizz year-round and reclaiming its place at the table, rather than hauling it out solely as a celebratory totem for birthdays, anniversaries, and the perfunctory New Year's Eve toast, but we've also internalized an important lesson. In short, sparkling wine is a form of wine like any other, and as such, it reflects the particularities of the places where it is grown and made.

To put it another way, we've finally paved the way for a deeper appreciation of sparkling wine as an expression of what the French call terroir.

Though impossible to translate directly, the term refers to the quasi-mystical notion that, as an agricultural product, wine should convey something about its geographical origin—whether it be a particular region or village or even an individual parcel of vines. Long considered the benchmark for greatness in still wine, terroir rarely factored into the conversation surrounding bubbles, as if the presence of a little carbonation inherently disqualified the wine from being taken seriously.

Not so anymore. With this reclamation has emerged a whole new kaleidoscope of sparkling regions and styles, made according to an array of different techniques, of which the so-called Champagne or traditional method is just one example. Rather than reduce this wonderful rainbow of expressions to the shabby catchall of "Champagne alternatives," we're now free to examine them each on their own merits.

Today's wine lover can choose, for example, between a single-vineyard grower Champagne (see page 24), bottled by one of the area's small independent producers, and a hazy bottle of pétillant-naturel (aka pét-nat), the natural wine movement's signature contribution to the genre. There's an endless assortment of world-class Italian sparkling wine to explore, from the cool-climate charms of Franciacorta to the revival of old-school, bottle-fermented Lambrusco.

This doesn't even begin to scratch the surface. Enthusiasts have rediscovered the farmhouse traditions of little-known French regions, like Bugey and Gaillac, and have witnessed an explosion of cutting-edge Spanish Cava and German Sekt. Even England, of all places, is making top-notch examples (just in time for Brexit), to say nothing of the influx of ambitious New World efforts from California, Oregon, and the entire Southern Hemisphere. Sparkling wine even comes in cans.

How to Use This Book

To develop a sense of context for this brave new world of bubbly isn't easy. The breakneck speed at which the old hierarchy has crumbled can't help but inspire a sense of whiplash.

The following chapters aim to put the current sparkling wine renaissance into a clear cultural perspective. In addition to outlining the basics of how it is made and debunking a handful of lingering myths about the category (no, you don't need to serve it in a traditional Champagne flute, and yes, it ages in bottle just like the still stuff), the main sparkling regions you can expect to encounter on wine lists and store shelves across the United States are covered.

Broken down by country, these regional overviews encompass all you need to understand about each area's place within the wider sparkling wine zeitgeist, including its history, its array of styles, and a list of "Producers to Know." Each chapter concludes with "The Wine List," a tightly curated selection of bottles meant to represent a cross section of what the area offers drinkers today, all chosen with value to the consumer in mind. Value is always relative, so for specific price points refer to the following chart.

$	Under $25
$$	$25 to $50
$$$	$50 or more

To that end, it would be wise to issue a brief disclaimer. The sparkling wine universe we now inhabit is every bit as vast and freewheeling as that of wine itself. Now that distinctive examples can be found every-where on Earth—or at least everywhere wine is made—it would be impossible to account for every last outpost on the fizzy map.

By necessity, then, the scope will be limited to those parts of the globe that already boast rich sparkling wine legacies (many of which are still in the midst of evolving) and to the emerging zones that demonstrate the greatest potential for carving out twenty-first-century traditions of their own. Rather than an encyclopedic overview, treat this book as a practical field guide to the main people and places driving progress forward.

In that spirit, let the pages empower you to drink as weirdly and wildly as possible, taking in the full range of sparkling wine idioms suddenly at our disposal. The fact that such a guide could exist in the first place is a testament to how many new horizons are now ours to explore.

How Sparkling Wine Is Made

For such a complex category, the basic science behind bubbly wine is actually quite simple. When yeast eats sugar (that is, the fermentation process), two by-products occur: alcohol, of course, and carbon dioxide (CO_2). When this CO_2 gets trapped inside a sealed enclosure, the pressure builds and voilà—a sparkling wine is born.

The complicated part is determining exactly how and where that process takes place. Through one fermentation or two? In the tank or directly within the bottle? Though these distinctions might seem nitpicky, they couldn't matter more.

With that in mind, there are three main methods of sparkling wine production. Together they account for virtually all of the sparkling wines of the world: the traditional or Champagne method (also called the "classical" method); the Charmat or tank method; and the ancestral method, also known as the méthode ancestrale.

You might be wondering why you should care about such "shop talk" in the first place. Presumably you bought this book because you like drinking wine, not making it. But in the same way that it's empowering to know whether a specific pinot noir was aged in new or neutral oak, the ability to contextualize terms such as *dosage* and *autolysis* or to distinguish between primary and secondary fermentation in bottle opens up a whole new realm of appreciation—all the better to help you navigate your way through today's bewildering maze of fizzy options and drink more of what you like. The fact is, each of these methods yields a radically different result, impacting everything from taste and texture to the size and shape of the bubbles. So when it comes to understanding stylistic diversity in sparkling wine—what makes one example taste different from the next—the technical details count for an awful lot.

Beyond giving you a sense of what to expect when you pop the cork (or crown cap, as the case may be), the following three methods also offer a useful framework for classifying the various sparkling wines of the world. As an organizing principle, the chapters that follow will be divided not just by region but also by technique, so let's brush up on the basics before diving deeper.

Traditional or Champagne Method

The méthode champenoise or traditional method (méthode tradition-nelle), sometimes also referred to as the classical method (metodo classico), has long served as the gold standard for premium sparkling wine production. For this reason, it has been adopted virtually every-where bubbly is made, from northern Italy (see Franciacorta, page 61), Spain (see Cava, page 93), Germany, and Austria (where it's called Sekt; see page 117) to California (see page 141) and beyond, to say nothing of the varied French sparklers that fall under the crémant umbrella (see crémant du Jura, crémant d'Alsace, and so on).

But it was in the chilly cellars of Champagne that the technique was first invented and perfected, born out of a sense of climactic necessity. In such northerly latitudes, grapes historically struggled to ripen, yielding harsh, acidic still wines. Over time, the Champenois discovered that with a little human skill these raw materials could be coaxed into something magical. The key to this alchemy involves creating a secondary fermen-tation directly inside the bottle by injecting the base wine with a solution of sugar and yeast known as the liqueur de tirage. When the bottle is resealed, the added sugar and yeast continue to ferment, and what was once a still wine becomes a sparkling one.

From here the winemaker's job is hardly over. After the secondary fermentation is complete, the wine is left in contact with the resulting sediment of dead yeast cells (lees) for an extended period, often up to several years. During this prolonged time-out, it gains richness and texture via a chemical reaction called autolysis, during which it soaks up the nutty, savory, brioche-like quality that is a hallmark of fine Champagne. The longer the wine ages in contact with the lees, the more of that rich autolytic character it will ultimately absorb. Only at the end of this long sentence in the bottle is the wine deemed ready to be disgorged (the process of removing the sediment from the bottle), re-corked, and shipped off to market. This is also the stage where the winemaker might choose to add dosage, a mix of sugar and base wine traditionally used in Champagne to balance the wine's sharp acidity. That said, contemporary taste increasingly favors lower levels of sweetness—hence, the rise of zéro dosage sparklers not only in Champagne but all over the globe.

There are quicker, easier ways to make sparkling wine. But the time, energy, and painstaking effort involved in the traditional method yield what many consider the most complex, elegant, and age-worthy form of fizz. And while Champagne remains the emblematic example, winemakers are now applying the technique all over the world with an eye toward expressing their own unique sense of place.

Charmat, Marinotti, or Tank Method

Sometimes all we want is the bubbly version of a beach read, not *Gravity's Rainbow*. It was for those occasions that the tank method was designed. Also known as the Charmat or Marinotti method (long story short, an Italian invented it in 1895, but a Frenchman updated and patented it twelve years later), the technique gets a bad rap among wine geeks because of its widespread role in churning out bubbles on an industrial scale. At the same time, however, the method produces some of the world's most popular sparkling wines, including that perennial fan favorite, Prosecco.

Significantly less costly and labor-intensive than the traditional method, the Charmat method enacts the secondary fermentation in massive pressurized tanks, to which sugar and yeast are added in bulk. Do the results lack the depth and complexity of their traditional-method counter-parts? Absolutely. But to fault Charmat wines for lacking Champagne's seriousness misses the point. As a technique, it's far better suited to preserving a wine's underlying fruit flavors. You get none of the yeasty, savory autolytic qualities of Champagne, but that's often a good thing. For example, when it comes to certain delicate, aromatic grapes (such as Prosecco's glera), Charmat channels the straightforward drink-me-now freshness that audiences everywhere have come to crave.

CHAMPAGNE (OR TRADITIONAL) METHOD

PICKED & PRESSED

PRIMARY FERMENTATION RESULTS IN A STILL BASE WINE

ADDITION OF LIQUEUR DE TIRAGE (SUGAR AND YEAST) CREATES SECONDARY FERMENTATION DIRECTLY IN BOTTLE

WINE IS AGED IN BOTTLE BEFORE DISGORGING, RE-CORKING, AND PACKAGING

CHARMAT (OR TANK) METHOD

PICKED & PRESSED

PRIMARY FERMENTATION RESULTS IN A STILL BASE WINE

ADDITION OF LIQUEUR DE TIRAGE CREATES SECONDARY FERMENTATION IN STAINLESS-STEEL TANK

WINE IS FILTERED AND CLARIFIED TO REMOVE SEDIMENT, BOTTLED AND PACKAGED

ANCESTRAL METHOD

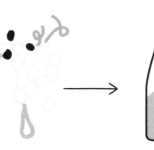

PICKED & PRESSED

THE PARTIALLY FERMENTED MUST (GRAPE JUICE) IS BOTTLED AND SEALED

PRIMARY FERMENTATION FINISHES IN THE BOTTLE, TRAPPING CO_2 (NO SECONDARY FERMENTATION)

WINE CAN BE DISGORGED OR LEFT CLOUDY (WINEMAKER'S CHOICE) AND SEALED UNDER A CROWN CAP

Ancestral Method

Most of us were first introduced to the ancestral method through the viral sensation of cloudy, gently sparkling pétillant-naturel, the natural wine movement's signature breed of bubbly. As its name indicates, the technique signals a conscious throwback to an earlier era of sparkling wine production. In fact, in the areas of France and Italy where it first originated, it predates the Champagne method by centuries.

Unlike the traditional and Charmat methods, both of which require a secondary fermentation, the ancestral method involves bottling and sealing the wine before the initial fermentation has finished. The released carbon dioxide gets caught in the bottle, imparting a soft foam of bubbles and occasionally a faint kiss of sweetness (thanks to the residual sugar that hasn't been converted into alcohol). Inspired by this tradition, today's deliberately funky ancestral method wines have attracted attention far and wide, playing up their lo-fi appeal at a time when we're obsessed with the reclamation of bygone styles.

A Brief Word on Carbonation

Okay, okay. So there's actually a fourth method of sparkling wine production that warrants a quick mention, even if most of the wines it generates command little respect. Still wine can be turned bubbly through a direct injection of CO_2, not unlike the effects of a giant SodaStream. In fairness, the technique would be entirely discounted if it weren't for that inexpensive summertime staple, Vinho Verde (see page 103), Portugal's contribution to the canon of low-key poolside wines. A handful of progressive producers (including the Scholium Project in California) have recently given the method a second look, filtering it through a prism of postmodern hipster irony, but generally speaking, it occupies the lowest rung of the fizzy totem pole.

Is Sparkling Wine Natural Wine?

For such an innocent-sounding term, *natural wine* has been thrust into the center of a controversy that has roiled the wine world for decades. If you ever want to rile up a wine geek, regardless of which side of the divide they identify with, just ask for a working definition for the concept.

Despite all the controversy natural wine courts, the "minimal intervention" belief system on which it is built adheres to a single straightforward principle: the most authentic wine is that which has had the least "done" to it in the way of chemical or technical manipulation. Now the foundation of an international movement, this ideal translates to a commonly accepted set of practices, including farming organically or biodynamically and, in the cellar, avoiding interfering with the wine-making process to the greatest extent possible. Hence, the popular naturalist mantra that the winemaker's role is simply to "let the wine make itself."

Sounds pretty uncomplicated in theory, doesn't it? Well, in practice, it's anything but. Even if we all agree that a wine shouldn't be too heavily marked by the winemaker's hand, allowing its underlying sense of terroir to shine through, it's not always clear just how hands-off that approach ought to be. Is it okay to add a little bit of stabilizing sulfur before bottling to prevent oxidation? If so, how much? This "natural or not" debate becomes all the more tricky, moreover, when it comes to sparkling wine.

After all, by definition, sparkling wine production (almost always) requires an extra level of technological intervention. Out of all the wine styles of the world, it is arguably the most process-driven and technically demanding. This goes a long way toward explaining why pét-nat—produced by the ancestral method of fermentation (see page 10)—has become natural wine's preferred form of bubbly. By bottling the wine while the primary fermentation is still taking place, effectively allowing it to carbonate itself as it's in the process of being made, there is no need to create a secondary fermentation. In other words, the fewer the steps, the better.

Certain critics even claim that, given the extra manipulation (in the form of added sugar and yeast) involved in their creation, wines made in the Champagne method cannot truly qualify as natural. In her book *Natural Wine,* author Isabelle Legeron explicitly excludes Champagne, noting that "making truly natural Champagne is currently illegal" in light of the "requirement to add yeast to start off the second fermentation in the bottle."

Nevertheless, that hasn't prevented forward-thinking winemakers in Champagne and elsewhere from trying to work in a more natural way in the cellar. For instance, some have started experimenting with using grape juice from the same vintage in place of commercial sugar to kick-start the secondary fermentation. For the purposes of this book, "natural" never suggests a binary proposition. As in all complex philo-sophical questions, naturalness exists along a continuum. Surely one can acknowledge the difference between, say, a chemically farmed wine from one of the large Champagne houses—fermented with laboratory yeasts and added sugar and produced on a mass-market scale—and the work of a small farmer who grows her own grapes according to biodynamic principles and takes the utmost care in the cellar to craft transparent sparkling wines that ring true to their place of origin.

13

Natural or not, that's simply the goal of great winemaking—and sparkling wine is no exception. For that reason, a high percentage of the spar-kling wines recommended in the pages that follow lay claim to some sort of naturalist street cred. Whether their winemakers consciously adopt that label or not, the objective remains the same—naturally.

Dispelling the Myths about Sparkling Wine

What is it about bubbles? No other form of alcohol has appealed more powerfully to the popular imagination. And yet all the romantic symbolism associated with the genre has always distracted from a deeper understanding of what's in the glass. The only thing that seemed to matter was that festive *pop*! of the cork.

This long history of misconceptions is underscored by one fundamental false notion: that sparkling wine isn't wine per se. Various reasons for this bias exist, and there will be plenty of time to unpack them over the course of this book. For now, in the interest of getting a start on that task, here are seven major sparkling wine myths that deserve to be cleared up once and for all.

It should be served in a Champagne flute.

First, no matter the style, drink what you like in whatever vessel you please. But if you want to get the full experience out of your bubbly, you might consider taking your cues from the latest wave of sommeliers, who have waged a campaign to ditch the traditional flute in favor of a standard white-wine glass. The wider the brim, the thinking goes, the better you'll be able to appreciate the wine's inherent flavors and aromas.

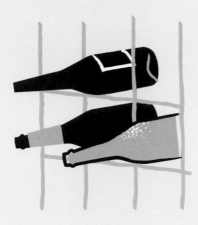

It should be drunk young (that is, it doesn't age).

Most sparkling wines—and to be honest, most wines, period—are built to be popped and poured as young as possible, highlighting their fruit and freshness. What many drinkers don't realize, though, is that certain sparklers improve with time like any of the world's celebrated still wines. Great Champagne is the most obvious illustration; with age, it acquires an incredibly nutty, umami-rich complexity, with a softer, lusher sort of effervescence. But the famous French region claims no monopoly on longevity. From the chiseled, densely textured brut chenin blancs from the Loire Valley to an influx of artisanal Cavas (to name just a few), the market is overflowing with bubbly that benefits from aging.

It should be served ice-cold.

Lukewarm sparkling wine is nobody's idea of a good time, but chilling the stuff beyond recognition is in many ways just as offensive. While all sparkling wine will benefit from a quick dunk in the ice bucket, serving it too cold mutes the wine's flavors and aromas. As with most white wines, its message typically comes across much more clearly at just below cellar temperature (a thirty-minute stint in the fridge will usually do the trick). So unless you're dining alfresco on a sweltering August afternoon, there's no need to keep your bottle on ice throughout the entire meal.

It should only be served as an aperitif.

It is a truth universally acknowledged that there is no greater predinner palate cleanser than a glass of something crisp, brisk, and bubbly. This perfunctory role, however, has largely excluded sparkling wine from taking a seat at the dinner table. That's a shame, because to limit your fizzy consumption to cocktail hour means missing out on some of the wine world's most versatile pairings. As a rule, cleansing acidity and effervescence equal insane compatibility with food, and there's a sparkling wine for every culinary situation, whether Brut Nature (that is, no added sugar) Champagne with sushi, pét-nat with a platter of char siu (Chinese barbecued pork), or dry Lambrusco with a slice of pepperoni pie.

It's just for holidays and special occasions.

Even as we're beginning to appreciate sparkling wine as more than an accessory to celebration, in the minds of most Americans it's still synonymous with special occasions. The vast majority of our bubbly consumption takes place during that gluttonous interval between Thanksgiving and New Year's. Much of the rest, it's safe to assume, gets drunk on birthdays, anniversaries, and Valentine's Day. This probes to the heart of our fraught relationship with the genre. But now more than ever, there's no reason to wait. Not only is Champagne being poured much more casually in today's top restaurants but we also have access to a whole new raft of informal sparkling wines (beyond that go-to bottle of Prosecco) that beg to be enjoyed just because.

Fizz is fizz is fizz. (It's all the same.)

Nobody would ever conflate a Tuscan Chianti with a Napa cabernet just because both are red. Ditto a New Zealand sauvignon blanc and an Italian pinot grigio. So why do we keep treating the entire effervescent family of wines like de facto substitutes for one another? Prosecco inhabits a completely different universe of flavor and texture compared with Champagne, which differs radically from Cava, which has nothing to do with pét-nat, Lambrusco, or Vinho Verde. And how boring it would be if otherwise.

The good stuff doesn't come cheap.

We can thank Champagne—or rather, the marketing savvy of the Champenois—for the ongoing belief that sparkling wine is, by definition, a luxury product. This idea has no place in today's democratic world of sparkling wine, which overflows with affordable bottles from areas far and wide. For one, the modern pét-nat boom has seriously accelerated that evolution, but there have always been bubbly options for all budgets beyond the usual suspects of Cava and Prosecco. You can find them on nearly every page of this book.

France

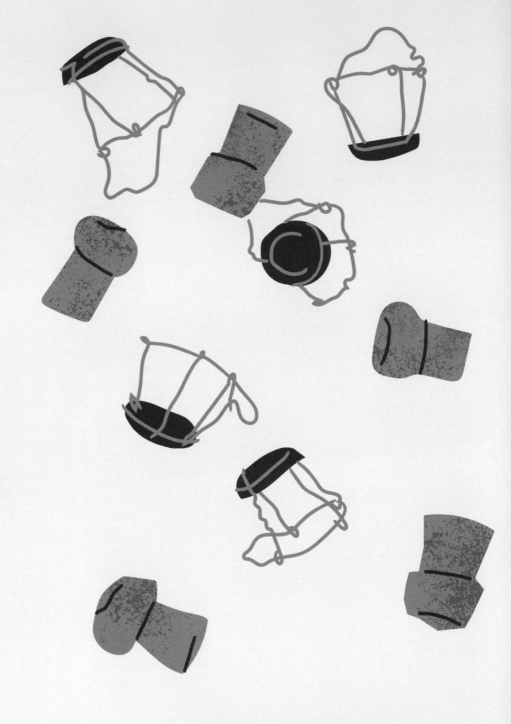

Champagne

Where else could this story begin but in Champagne? Ever since 1693, when, according to local legend, a Benedictine monk by the name of Dom Pérignon first invented the stuff, the French region has been famous for producing the world's most influential and widely imitated sparkling wine.

As any Champagne lover will tell you, there's a good reason why. Those storied vineyards outside the village of Reims give birth to fizzy wines of incomparable intrigue and beauty that could come from nowhere but the limestone soils of France's northernmost (and therefore coldest) viticultural zone. The original benchmark for sparkling wine greatness, Champagne's classic cool-climate combo of chiseled acidity, chalky minerality, and savory complexity set a standard against which all other forms of bubbly would be forced to measure up.

Of course, the modern dismantling of that tenet provides the point of departure for this book. But even if we no longer feel the need to measure all sparkling wine against Champagne's yardstick, it would be next to impossible to acquire any meaningful sense of today's ever-evolving bubbly landscape without first coming to terms with the original benchmark that defined our understanding of the category from the start.

Champagne Basics: A Primer

Surprisingly, given its iconic nature, most drinkers never bothered to pay attention to the details that make Champagne what it is—its main grapes and subregions, its production methods and traditional template of styles—until just a few years ago. So the first step toward grasping Champagne's versatility as a wine necessarily involves taking a closer look at the basic building blocks of its identity, starting with its classic mix of grapes.

Setting aside a few quirky heirloom examples such as arbane and petit meslier, which you'll rarely encounter in your glass, three major varieties form Champagne's holy trinity. You might be surprised to learn that two of them—pinot noir and pinot meunier—are red. (Yes, you can make white wine from red grapes, and the Champenois coined the word for the style, as we'll see.) Along with chardonnay, the region's major white, each plays an important role in delineating Champagne's stylistic spectrum, whether featured solo or combined in blends. Here's a quick breakdown of the categories.

Blanc de Blancs: French for "white of whites," any Champagne labeled blanc de blancs almost always consists entirely of chardonnay. It's typically the most elegant, bright, and mineral-driven expression of Champagne.

Blanc de Noirs: Made strictly from dark-skinned grapes (either 100 percent pinot noir or pinot meunier, or any combination of the two), blanc de noirs represents the polar opposite or inverse of a blanc de blancs Champagne. By fermenting the clear grape juice off of its skins, the result is a white wine that carries a little extra red-fruited flesh on its bones.

Nonvintage: A blend of base wines from several different vintages, the nonvintage (NV) category accounts for approximately 75 percent of the region's annual production. Historically, the nonvintage bottling within a Champagne brand's lineup served as a calling card of sorts for telegraphing a specific house style.

Prestige cuvée: A prestige cuvée typically represents the top-of-the-line vintage bottling of a Champagne house (think Louis Roederer's Cristal or Moët & Chandon's Dom Pérignon). Traditionally considered the pinnacle of quality for the region, prestige cuvées are certainly the priciest and also the most susceptible to luxury branding. Broadcasting that fact, they tend to undergo unusually long periods of lees aging in bottle, often upward of eight years.

Rosé: There are two ways to make pink Champagne. As its name, rosé d'assemblage, would suggest, the most common method entails blending a small amount of red wine into a white base wine. Rosé de saignée, or macerated Champagne, involves keeping the red grape skins in contact with the juice for a short period of time, during which the pigment leaches (or "bleeds off," as the French say) into the wine.

Single vineyard: Unlike most Champagnes, which are blended from several different parts of the region, a single-vineyard Champagne is a snapshot of a specific individual site. Though certain examples of these Champagnes have been well known for decades—Krug's legendary Clos du Mesnil immediately springs to mind—the style has become increasingly popular as the region embraces a more terroir-driven, site-sensitive ethos.

Vintage: The product of a single year's harvest, vintage Champagne comprises just 5 percent of the region's total production. Only produced in excellent years, it's almost always more expensive than nonvintage and must be aged for at least three years on the lees (as opposed to just fifteen months for NV Champagne).

A pro tip: Be sure to remember these terms, as they'll continue to pop up even outside the wines of Champagne itself. A testament to the outsized influence of Champagne's legacy, this basic framework has been adopted by sparkling wine regions the world over.

The Shifting Image of Champagne

More than a beverage, Champagne is a symbol. From "the whisperings and the champagne and the stars" of Jay Gatsby's garden parties to Biggie at "the back of the club, sippin' Moët," it has forever been synonymous with the good life.

That didn't happen by accident. Ever since the late eighteenth century, when Champagne merchants deliberately advertised the wine's royal pedigree to cater to France's growing middle-class market, Champagne's identity has been inseparable from this aspirational narrative. Fast-forward to the present and it's easy to draw a straight line between this early history and Beyoncé notoriously dumping a pricy bottle of Armand de Brignac (the brand she and Jay-Z acquired in 2014 for an undisclosed sum) into her Jacuzzi.

This genius for self-promotion has preserved Champagne's status as the world's most famous sparkling wine, widely imitated yet utterly inimitable. Ironically, though, Champagne is famous in the same way that Rolex or

Gucci is famous—as a high-end brand. The quintessential "special occasion" wine, it exists in the popular imagination as more of a celebratory totem than a wine of place.

But as happens to any symbol over time, the meaning of Champagne has started to change—radically, in fact. Within the last two decades, a revolution has come to this traditionally commercial region, upending its longstanding balance of power and raising serious questions about the way its wines are produced, distributed, served, and enjoyed.

Rarely does a place as historic as Champagne undergo such a major cultural overhaul. But the transformation that continues to redefine it in the wake of the uprising by the region's small-scale growers has ushered in a new golden age of Champagne consumption. Never before have we been able to enjoy such a wide range of styles and expressions, nor has quality ever been higher.

The Grower Champagne Revolution

Drinkers tend to treat Champagne as a luxury good probably because the region has always done the same. For centuries, Champagne has been dominated by the grandes marques (major brands), such as Moët & Chandon, Taittinger, and Veuve Clicquot. They have built a multibillion-dollar industry on their ability to deliver a consistent product to a vast audience of drinkers across the globe.

Traditionally, their approach involved purchasing vast quantities of grapes from thousands of growers scattered across the region and blending together multiple wines from vintages past and present to arrive at a signature house style. In this way, for much of the region's history, the art of Champagne production took place in the cellar rather than in the vineyard.

This explains why, come rain or shine, that ubiquitous bottle of yellow-label Veuve Clicquot tastes almost exactly the same. While useful from a branding perspective, this mass-market formula lacks the qualities we normally look for in the great wines of the world: the unique stamp of vintage and vineyard.

Starting in the 1990s, a handful of small growers rallied around a game-changing question: What if, rather than selling off their grapes to the corporate Champagne houses, they made their own estate-grown and bottled wines? What would Champagne look like if it were reimagined as a wine of terroir, crafted on a human scale by real people with the goal of reflecting the identity of a specific village or even a single parcel of vines?

Convinced that it's impossible to make great wine without healthy grapes, many of the area's growers have started farming organically and biodynamically, practices that were virtually nonexistent here even twenty years ago. Their efforts are all the more heroic in light of the region's damp, unforgiving climate, where grapes are susceptible to rot, mildew, and all manner of ills.

At first, very few of these so-called grower Champagnes trickled into the US market. But thanks to the work of several boutique importers who brought the first examples to US shores, the category has since exploded. Now a necessary fixture on restaurant wine lists with even the slightest alternative bent, these artisanal examples have taught a new generation of drinkers to recognize Champagne as an actual wine—one that just happens to contain bubbles.

That's not to suggest that "grower" necessarily means better. The large Champagne houses produce plenty of exquisite wines. (No self-respecting wine lover would ever turn up their nose at a glass of Bollinger, Billecart-Salmon, or Krug.) The point is that the grower movement has introduced a whole new perspective on Champagne, shifting the emphasis from product to place.

Not only have we started discussing Champagne in the language of wine, evaluating it in terms of criteria such as soil type, farming practices, and vintage variation, but the way we're interacting with it has evolved as well. If you order Champagne in a restaurant today, chances are it will be served to you in a white-wine glass as opposed to the once customary flute—all the better, the thinking goes, to taste and smell what's in the glass.

The Rise of Brut Nature Champagne

As you begin to explore the alternative universe of grower Champagne, you'll start to notice a pattern: in effect, a spate of bottles labeled "extra brut" or "brut nature" (and occasionally "brut zéro" or "pas dosé"). These terms designate an increasingly popular style of Champagne to which extremely little (if any) sugar, or dosage, has been added before bottling.

Dosage has traditionally been viewed as a critical measure to help balance (at times) the astringent acidity of Champagne. But today, many growers have come to view the practice with a certain amount of skepticism. For one, thanks to rising ripeness levels (courtesy of climate change), it's simply not as necessary as it was in the past. But to a deeper extent, given Champagne's general shift toward site expression and specificity of place, the general consensus is that, while dosage can help round out a wine's sharp angles, too much of it risks obscuring terroir.

For this reason, the brut nature category has become highly fashionable among the latest generation of Champagne purists. Powerfully mineral and savory, this new crop of bracingly dry renditions has helped to push Champagne one step closer to being treated like any other serious wine.

PRODUCERS TO KNOW

Agrapart et Fils	J. Vignier
A. Margaine	Lahèrte Frères
André Beaufort	Larmandier-Bernier
Bérêche et Fils	Laurent Bénard
Cédric Bouchard	Marie Courtin
Champagne Aubry	Mouzon Leroux & Fils
Champagne Marguet	Pierre Gerbais
Champagne Rupert-Leroy	Pierre Gimmonet
Champagne Savart	Pierre Moncuit
Champagne Suenen	Pierre Paillard
Champagne Tarlant	Pierre Peters
Chartogne-Taillet	Ployez-Jacquemart
Christophe Mignon	R. Pouillon & Fils
Emmanuel Brochet	Ulysse Colin
Flavien Nowack	Val Frison
Jacques Lassaigne	Vilmart & Cie
Jérôme Prévost	Vouette & Sorbée
J. L. Vergnon	

A Quick Guide to the Subregions

If the main legacy of the grower movement has been to insert place back into the conversation about Champagne, it follows that, like any other area, Champagne is increasingly being understood in the context of its five specific subregions. Each of these divisions roughly corresponds to its own set of styles and blends of the region's three major grapes.

Montagne de Reims

Curling northward just above the village of Épernay, Montagne de Reims is a celebrated source of pinot noir, giving richer, spicier wines in the classic blanc de noirs style.

Vallée de la Marne

Traditionally typecast as a workhorse grape to fatten up blends, pinot meunier has recently acquired a kind of cult status among wine geeks thanks to a handful of grower-producers in the Vallée de la Marne, where it represents a local specialty. On its own, the grape makes robust, food-friendly wines with fleshy fruit and big personalities. Despite pinot meunier stealing the limelight, plenty of chardonnay and pinot noir are planted here as well.

Côte des Blancs

Just south of Épernay, the aptly named Côte des Blancs is planted almost exclusively with chardonnay, which reaches a maximum of elegance in the area's chalky limestone soils. It's here that many of the region's greatest all-chardonnay blanc des blancs bottlings call home, such as Krug's famous single-vineyard Clos du Mesnil.

Côte de Sézanne

Located due south of the Côte des Blancs, the Côte de Sézanne, with its preponderance of chardonnay vines, is often viewed as a mini version of the former. Its wines tend to be riper and slightly lower in acidity than the filigreed expression of the grape found farther north. Still, in the right hands, the area is capable of wines that stand toe to toe with any of its neighbor's finest.

MONTAGNE
DE REIMS

VALLÉE DE
LA MARNE

CÔTE DES
BLANCS

CÔTE DE
SÉZANNE

THE AUBE

The Aube

Also known as the Côte des Bar, the
Aube is Champagne's southernmost and
least historically renowned subregion.
Formerly considered a source of cheap
blending grapes for the big houses, the
area is now staking its claim as the new
capital of Champagne's naturalist avant-
garde. Pinot noir has a long history here,
but you can expect some racy, mineral
chardonnay as well.

The Wine List

It's impossible to reduce a region as complex and evolving as Champagne to a user-friendly roundup of options. Though far from definitive, the following bottles offer a solid place to start.

Champagne Aubry Premier Cru Brut ($$)

Always one of Champagne's top bargains, this crowd-pleaser from the Montagne de Reims's Aubry brothers offers up far more complexity— thanks, in part, to the high percentage of older reserve wine used in the blend—than its modest price tag would suggest.

R. Pouillon & Fils Réserve Brut ($$)

Based in the town of Mareuil-sur-Aÿ, Fabrice Pouillon is making some of the most impressive terroir-focused, biodynamic wines in the Vallée de la Marne. Here, the red-skinned grapes (pinot noir and pinot meunier) set the tone structurally—firm and big-boned with hints of earthiness, it cleans up nicely with a wash of gingerroot spice.

Champagne Savart "L'Ouverture" Premier Cru Brut ($$)

Grower Frédéric Savart's entry-level (but by no means basic) "L'Ouverture" cuvée, made entirely of pinot noir from the village of Écueil, combines that grape's textural density with rose-petal aromatics and a bite of Japanese pear.

Val Frison "Goustan" Blanc de Noirs Brut Nature ($$$)

Valérie Frison's skill with pinor noir comes across in this textbook take on the blanc de noirs style. Assembled from three different vineyards in the Côte des Bar—Les Clos de la Côte, La Chevêtrée, and La Ville—it's a powerful, red-fruited Champagne with serious intensity on the palate.

Vouette & Sorbée "Fidèle" Extra Brut ($$$)

Bertrand Gautherot, of the cult Vouette & Sorbée estate, produces this stellar blanc de noirs with pinot noir from the experimental hotbed of the Aube. Lees aged for twenty months, it wears its extra brut designation proudly, with a lean chalkiness and bright acidity.

Laurent Bénard La Clé des Sept Arpents Extra Brut ($$$)

Home to the legendary houses of Bollinger, Philipponnat, and Billecart-Salmon, the famous Vallée de la Marne village of Mareuil-sur-Aÿ is also where husband-and-wife team Laurent and Michelle Bénard-Pitois have organically farmed their small holdings of vines for over twenty-five years. Two-thirds pinot meunier with chardonnay, and pinot noir filling in the rest, this vintage-dated Champagne skews toward the denser side of the spectrum.

Chartogne-Taillet "Cuvée Sainte Anne" Brut ($$)

After apprenticing with Anselme Selosse, the great pioneer of organic viticulture in Champagne, the young Alexandre Chartogne returned to his family winery in 2006 to craft some of the region's most sought-after wines. Even at the basic nonvintage level, his "Cuvée Sainte Anne" Brut—taken from a tapestry of vineyards in the village of Merfy—never disappoints, with its flavors of Gala apple and a long, umami-filled finish.

Lahèrte Frères "Rosé de Meunier" Extra Brut ($$)

Embodying all that's bold and beautiful about the pinot meunier grape, this now-iconic rosé Champagne from grower Aurélien Laherte pours a deeper hue of pink than most, suggesting the unexpected depth and concentration contained within. To put it bluntly, this is as good as pink Champagne gets.

J. L. Vergnon "Eloquence" Grand Cru Extra Brut ($$$)

Hailed by leading Champagne critic Peter Liem as "one of the top estates in the Côte des Blancs today," the family-run house of Jean-Louis Vergnon has been estate-bottling its own wine since 1985. This 100 percent chardonnay bottling is sourced from thirty-plus-year-old vines planted (mostly) in the grand cru of Le Mesnil-sur-Oger in the heart of the Côte des Blancs.

Jacques Lassaigne "Les Vignes de Montgueux" Blanc de Blancs Extra Brut ($$)

If you want to understand the elegance and finesse that supposedly define the blanc de blancs style, look no further than this racy, filigreed example from Jacques Lassaigne, one of the Aube's true masters of chardonnay. His most basic bottling, "Les Vignes de Montgueux," comes from nine different sites in its namesake village, offering a big-picture view of Montgueux's clay- and chalk-dominated soils.

Crémant
French Bubbles beyond Champagne

Exacting as they tend to be in such matters, the French have a specific word to describe sparkling wines made in the Champagne method from areas other than Champagne. That word is *crémant,* and for the curious sparkling wine drinker, it's a crucial one to know.

Today, the crémant umbrella extends over a diverse family of fizzy wines from several parts of France in a wide array of styles. But in the minds of most drinkers, crémant has meant one thing above all: a bargain. In the mood for Champagne but unable to afford the splurge? Cue the crémant. At least that's what the conventional wisdom always pre-scribed. By cutting and pasting the "Champagne method" onto cheaper real estate, the argument went, the category offered a close enough approximation to the genuine article minus the premium sticker shock. For decades, crémant served this sole purpose, and that's where the conversation ended. Little did it matter who, exactly, produced the crémant in question or where it happened to be made. Whether from the banks of the Loire or the mountains of Savoie, the basic selling point remained the same: Champagne-styled wines at charitably un-Champagne prices.

In fairness, crémant still delivers one of wine's great deals. As a rule, value in wine is discovered off the beaten path, in the overlooked peripheries and margins, and there could be no path more beaten than Champagne's. Comparatively, the quality you get for thirty dollars (and often less) from a top-notch crémant puts most entry-level brand-name Champagne to shame. But what if this timeworn comparison misses the point?

Until recently, all that anyone ever talked about with regard to crémant was its production method. But that logic omits a critical truth: when you apply the same technique in completely separate regions—with their wildly divergent climates, soil types, and native grape varieties—you wind up with sparkling wines with very different regional characters. Rather than measuring them against something they're not (Champagne), the best way to understand them is in light of their respective regions. For example, if we once looked to a bottle such as Domaine Bénédicte et Stéphane Tissot's crémant du Jura—a blend of chardonnay, pinot noir, and the hyperlocal poulsard grape—as a Champagne replacement, drinking it becomes all the more meaningful when we start to under-stand it as the unique expression of the Jura.

The same holds true for all of France's historic crémant-producing areas that, for the sake of convenience, can be roughly organized into four main camps along geographical lines: the north, the east, the center, and the south. Not every region that will be discussed uses the specific crémant designation, however. Certain areas with particularly deep sparkling wine histories—the Loire's Vouvray, for example, or Savoie's Seyssel—bottle their sparklers under their own specific regional names.

The North: Alsace

Nestled between the Vosges Mountains and the winding Rhine River, which carves out the German border, Alsace is one of France's classic wine regions—and, in many ways, its oddest. Having been tugged back and forth between the two countries for generations, the area's wine culture owes as much to France as it does to Germany. This curious bicultural heritage manifests on several fronts, including its unusual grab bag of grapes. Here, French examples such as pinot gris and pinot blanc share turf with traditionally Teutonic varieties, like riesling, gewürztraminer, and silvaner.

Though Alsace's claim to fame has rested on the status of its opulent, age-worthy whites, the region also produces a whole lot of bubbly. In fact, crémant d'Alsace accounts for nearly one-quarter of the region's total production. Given the prolific quantities of the stuff that Alsace churns out each year, quality tends to vary, but that hasn't prevented the French from prodigiously lapping it up. After Champagne, it's the second most popular sparkling wine in France.

Of all the crémant-producing areas, Alsace is arguably the hardest to pin down in terms of style. That's due, in no small part, to the wide assortment of grapes permitted in the blend, including pinot blanc (the most commonly used base variety), pinot gris, pinot noir, riesling, auxerrois (a simple local white typically reserved for blends), and chardonnay. Depending upon the percentage of each in any given example, as well as the intent of the winemaker, the results can range from zingy and thirst quenching to rich and complex.

While large industrial cooperatives dominate the region's fizzy output, many independent artisan estates also focus on crémant. That's especially true in recent years, as the region has attracted a growing cohort of fresh, natural-leaning talent. Despite its northerly location, Alsace is one of the driest and sunniest regions in France, making it among the country's great hotbeds of organic and biodynamic farming. That ample sunshine also means that grapes don't struggle as hard to ripen (at least, compared to Champagne), resulting in a proliferation of zéro dosage bottlings that represent the category's cutting edge.

Finally, a brief shout-out to one of France's best-kept sparkling secrets: crémant d'Alsace rosé. Made exclusively from pinot noir, when it's good, it's as good as pink fizz gets, displaying a chalky minerality and a rhubarb-like tang that the French have been all too happy to save for themselves.

PRODUCERS TO KNOW

Albert Boxler	Domaine Dirler-Cadé
Audrey et Christian Binner	Domaine Rieffel
Domaine Barmès-Buecher	Domaine Valentin Zusslin
Domaine Bechtold	Meyer-Fonné

The East: Burgundy, Jura, and Savoie

If you were to create a heat map of the wine world based solely on sommelier street cred, you might wonder what accounted for the small yet radioactive cluster burning along the eastern edge of France. Starting with the iconic region of Burgundy, but extending outward across the foothills of the Jura up through the rugged alpine territory of Savoie (Savoy), this bucolic corner of the country is home to some of France's most sought-after wines, including plenty of distinctive bubbly.

Though each region puts its own unique spin on the genre, a common thread runs through the sparkling wines produced in all three places. With their cool, marginal climates, they over-deliver on what drinkers want from their wine today: acidity, minerality, and the kind of spine-tingling freshness that comes across even in richer versions of the style. For this reason, of all the available options, these are the wines that tend to invoke the most frequent comparisons to Champagne. That said, each remains essential and unmistakable in its own right—not least of all, Burgundy.

Ever since the fourteenth century, when a bunch of Cistercian monks with a whole lot of time on their hands started demarcating the region's top vineyard sites, Burgundy's ethereal, mineral-driven pinot noirs and chardonnays have represented a rare archetype for greatness. Against that lofty backdrop, crémant de Bourgogne, as you'll read on the label, has traditionally functioned as more of a sideshow. But if it was once regarded as a crisp and simple prelude to the area's exalted whites and reds, Burgundy's signature sparkling wine is now carving out a more ambitious identity, incorporating both the classic regional varieties of pinot noir and chardonnay and such humbler kin as aligoté and gamay.

Though grapes destined for crémant are grown all across Burgundy, the category's historic heart of production typically bypasses the famed grand cru vineyards of the Côte d'Or, Burgundy's most illustrious sub-zone, favoring the cheaper real estate to the north and south. This geographic division translates to two distinct sparkling styles. The wines grown in the limestone soils of the Yonne, Burgundy's northern-most growing area, tend to showcase the same acidity and saline minerality found in the iconic whites of neighboring Chablis. Further south in the Côte Chalonnaise and Mâconnais areas, even including parts of Beaujolais, warmer weather and granitic soils impart a riper, rounder character. For a revealing exercise in contrasts, try the lean, angular examples from Clotilde Davenne or Bruno Dangin, both masters of the northern idiom, alongside the fuller-bodied southern crémant from Céline & Larent Tripoz.

Without the rampant price inflation that continues to engulf Burgundy, we might never have discovered the Jura, the pastoral wonderland of sleepy little villages that unfurls just an hour's drive east. No longer dismissed as Burgundy's "country cousin," the Jura now finds itself (however improbably) cast as one of the hottest things in wine. When the area first exploded from obscurity as the latest darling of the hipster wine circuit, it was the Jura's earthy yet translucent reds (from a mix of familiar grapes, like pinot noir, and native ones, like trousseau and the hyper-pale poulsard) and old-school oxidative whites (sourced from chardonnay and the local savagnin grapes and aged, like sherry, under a veil of yeast) that first hooked adventurous US drinkers.

Many of the winemakers responsible for this renaissance also make equally idiosyncratic fizz. Generally a touch riper than Burgundy's bottlings, crémant du Jura must be blended from at least 70 percent chardonnay, pinot noir, and trousseau, with poulsard and savagnin filling in the rest. Stylistically, they range from fun and fruit-driven to more serious, structured wines that spend extra time aging on the lees. The best examples of this elevated ethos—say, Domaine de Montbourgeau's chardonnay-based crémant from the village of l'Étoile—possess a rich, mouth-filling complexity, often with a subtle oxidative streak (think toasted nuts, baked apple) that channels the Jura's style of white winemaking into bubbly form. A handful of vibrant, minerally rosés are worth seeking out as well.

Perhaps it was inevitable that the industry love affair with the Jura would eventually spill over into neighboring Savoie, France's remote alpine region high up in the shadows of Mont Blanc. Once dismissed as simple après-ski wines for tourists to gulp down after a day on the slopes, Savoie's alpine whites have been embraced as perfect emblems of contemporary taste, walking a tightrope between textural depth and ripping acidity. That goes double for its high-altitude sparklers.

In addition to bottles bearing the regional crémant de Savoie designation, which typically highlight the bright, snappy character of the local jacquère grape, Savoie boasts two specific subregions dedicated to sparkling wine, and it's here that the style achieves its fullest potential. A historic center of Champagne-method bubbly based off the native molette and altesse grapes, the area of Seyssel enjoyed considerable fame during the nineteenth century for its sparkling "Seyssel mousseux." While there's not much of it to go around these days, the area still specializes in floral yet structured traditional-method wines that offer a glimpse of that pedigreed past.

For a look at Savoie's future, however, we need only consider the precipitous slopes of Ayse, where a single cult producer has catapulted the region to the heart of the avant-garde. All of Dominique Belluard's biodynamically farmed efforts to elevate the niche gringet grape achieve an almost impossible tension between richness, ripe orchard fruit (often with a hint of gingery spice), and electrifying acidity. It was the purity of his sparkling interpretations, however, that first landed him on the industry radar, including his flagship "Mont Blanc Brut Zéro," now a highly prized sommelier obsession, as well as the entry-level nonvintage "Les Perles du Mont Blanc." Grab either (or ideally, both), if you're lucky enough to spot a bottle.

39

PRODUCERS TO KNOW

Burgundy:	Savoie:
Céline & Laurent Tripoz	André et Michel Quenard
Clos des Vignes du Maynes	Domaine Belluard
Clotilde Davenne	Eugène Carrel
Domaine des Moirots	Lambert de Seyssel
Domaine Henri Naudin-Ferrand	Mathieu Apffel
François Mikulski	Jura: Bénédicte et Stéphane Tissot
Gabin et Félix Richoux	Domaine de Montbourgeau
Jean Noël Gagnard	Domaine des Marnes Blanches
Patrick Piuze (Val de Mer)	Domaine Labet
Jean Noël Gagnard	Domaine Rolet
Patrick Piuze (Val de Mer)	Peggy et Jean-Pascal Buronfosse
	Pierre Richard

The Center: The Loire

No region has embodied the core French belief in wine as an everyday staple more than the Loire, a vast tract of vineyard land that follows its namesake river over three hundred miles, from the district of Pouilly-Fumé, smack in the country's center, all the way west to Nantes, where it spills out into the Atlantic. The region's roll call of diverse bistro classics includes famous names such as Sancerre, Muscadet, and Chinon—all pillars of the Gallic table-wine tradition. But in a country as fizz-obsessed as France, that tradition would mean nothing without its bubbles.

Although ancestral-method pét-nat (see page 49) might generate most of the headlines these days, traditional-method sparklers (or "fine bulles," to locals) have been a fact of life in the Loire since the 1840s. As of the current century, the region's sparkling wines have never been better. Propelled by its newfound status as the capital of France's natural wine movement, the Loire has emerged as one of the country's great experimental laboratories, and the ensuing culture clash between time-tested classicism and radical innovation has reinvigorated its bubbly traditions across the board.

The broad category of wines labeled "crémant de Loire" can come from any of the Loire's three main sparkling subzones: Anjou, Saumur, and Touraine. Though the kitchen-sink list of permitted varieties includes everything from chardonnay and cabernet franc to pineau d'aunis, grolleau, and pinot noir, the star of the show is without question the chameleon-like chenin blanc. Chenin, as fans call it, excels in every possible stylistic register, from sweet to dry, still to sparkling. Even just within the latter camp, it encompasses a vast spectrum of its own.

The villages of Vouvray and Montlouis-sur-Loire, located on opposite sides of the Loire River ten miles east of Tours, act as stylistic book-ends for the category. Of the two, Vouvray is historically most famous and lays claim to the greater share of prestigious estates, including its twin titans, Domaines Huet and Foreau. The latter's richly textured Champagne-method chenins embodies a benchmark for the style. With its more open-ended identity, Montlouis has attracted a wave of younger (read natural-leaning) winemaking talent, thanks in no small part to the example set by its two luminaries, François Chidaine and Jacky Blot.

What makes chenin blanc so rewarding in its sparkling form is just how radically its flavors diverge from those of Champagne. Even when picked for sparkling wine, at typically lower ripeness levels, the grape's signature profile and texture—sometimes described as "waxy"—never fail to shine through. Courtesy of the area's classic tuffeau (limestone soil), the wines clean up nicely with enough acidity and minerality to satisfy the most die-hard terroir junkies. Depending on the intended style, some versions skew leaner and drier, with flavors of green apple, while others veer toward the unctuous, quince-like side of the spectrum. Either way, that unmistakable "chenin-ness," for lack of a better word, always abides.

PRODUCERS TO KNOW

Champalou	François et Julien Pinon
Château de Bois-Brinçon	Jacky Blot (La Taille aux Loups)
Denis Meunier	Jo Landron
Domaine Huet	Philippe Foreau (Domaine du Clos Naudin)
Domaine Sébastien Brunet	Pithon-Paillé
François Chidaine	

The South: Limoux, Saint-Péray, and Die

Bubbles don't immediately spring to mind when we imagine the South of France. We tend to think of sparkling wine as a northerly affair, and with good reason: the style naturally flourishes in cooler growing areas, where the struggle for ripeness brings the acid we all seek in the style. But that doesn't mean that the country is entirely bereft of bubbles once you follow the Rhône River below Lyon, the symbolic midpoint (for wine lovers, at least) between the chilly stoicism of the nord and the sun-dappled romanticism of the sud.

Far better known for its archetypal syrahs from famous villages such as Hermitage, Côte Rôtie, and Cornas, the northern Rhône Valley still manages to turn out a smattering of sparkling wine, in both the traditional and the ancestral method. (For now, the conversation will be limited to the former.)

Yet another nineteenth-century hub of méthode champenois winemaking, the village of Saint-Péray once enjoyed quite the reputation for its fizzy mousseux. (Napoléon numbered among its early admirers.) Made from the local marsanne and roussanne grapes, the examples you're likely to find today reward the curiosity required to seek them out, exhibiting a more southerly roundness and heft, often with flavors of yellow pear, hazelnuts, and thyme. Even more obscure, the vineyards of Pays Diois—a postage stamp of a region in the bucolic department of the Drôme, historically considered the gateway to Provence—have long produced clairette de Die, a semisweet, low-alcohol, peach-and-apricot-scented ancestral-method sparkler from clairette and muscat grapes. The region also produces a dry (to dry-ish) crémant de Die, using the same mix of grapes plus aligoté, that delivers similar high-toned floral aromas in a more substantial and savory package.

Pushing even deeper south, into the wilds of the Languedoc region that unfurls along France's Mediterranean coast, the ancient area of Limoux is almost entirely synonymous with sparkling wine. In fact, wine historians credit the region with producing the world's first example (see page 49).

For such a tiny area, Limoux offers the world a confounding array of sparkling wines, not even counting those made in the original ancestral method. Of these, the most visible is crémant de Limoux, a value-driven Champagne-method sparkler that reps the modern face of the region, with up to 90 percent of the blend coming from non-native grapes such as chardonnay and chenin blanc. More distinctive, if considerably rarer, Blanquette de Limoux refers to wines blended from at least 90 percent of the region's quirky, indigenous mauzac. If it tastes like it originates a world away from the northerly vineyards of Reims—tangy, mellow, and full of ripe melon and peach—then what you're tasting is true.

PRODUCERS TO KNOW

Alain Voge	Domaine Les Hautes Terres
Domaine Archard-Vincent	Domaine Martinolles
Domaine de Mouscaillo	

The Wine List

Domaine Valentin Zusslin Crémant d'Alsace Brut Zéro ($$)

The brother-and-sister team of Jean-Paul and Marie Zusslin have made waves for their entire range of whites, but their no-dosage biodynamic crémant—a mix of pinot auxerrois, chardonnay, and pinot gris—has been singled out for its leanness and raw sense of purity. Bottled without sulfur, its pristine fruit gives way to a cleansing froth of acidity. Look for the single-vineyard "Clos Liebenberg" expression as well.

Gabin et Félix Richoux Crémant de Bourgogne ($)

Burgundy's northern crémant style reaches a stylistic apotheosis in this lean, steely blanc de noirs. Taken from the Richoux family's highest-elevation pinot noir vines in the village of Irancy, just a stone's throw from Chablis, it's bright and lifted but concentrated in its green fruit flavors, with plenty of the seashell-like tidal-pool salinity for which the area's still whites are so famous.

Domaine des Marnes Blanches Crémant du Jura ($$)

Among the most promising talents to emerge out of the Jura's Sud Revermont area, Domaine des Marnes Blanches's Geraud and Pauline Fromont strive for a long and deeply textured cast of crémant. Though it's typically best to avoid such comparisons, if you happen to be in the market for the sort of sparkler that acts like fancy Champagne, this occupies the same rich-and-savory wheelhouse, with notes of almond paste, brown butter, and golden-apple skins.

Lambert de Seyssel "Le Petit Royal" Blanc de Blancs ($)

Bright, chamomile scented, and reminiscent of ripe quince, Lambert de Seyssel's entry-level sparkling Seyssel might be derived from the estate's younger vines, but it still delivers plenty of complexity. A classic mix of molette and altesse grapes (70 percent and 30 percent, respectively), it's the sort of hidden gem that rewards a willingness to stray from the beaten path.

Jacky et J. P. Blot (Domaine de La Taille aux Loups) Montlouis Brut Tradition ($$)

Sourced from organically farmed chenin vines that range from forty to eighty years old, Loire legend Jacky Blot's sparkling Montlouis is at once irreverent and iconic. Embodying the grape's classic combo of unctuousness and mouthwatering acidity, it's not just one of the Loire's great sparkling wines, but one of its great wines, period.

Alain Voge Saint-Péray "Les Bulles d'Alain" ($)

Posterity will remember the late Alain Voge for the rough-hewn beauty of his reds from the northern Rhône village of Cornas, but his estate also specializes in the little-known sparkling wines of Saint-Péray based on the marsanne grape. From thirty-year-old organic vines and aged for a minimum of three years on the lees (without any addition of dosage), this generously southern-styled sparkler leads with pear skin and sage-like spice with a warm, nutty fullness thanks to the extended time on the lees.

Taste the Rainbow

Pale/Translucent

António Lopes
Ribeiro Vinho Verde
"Biotite"

Light Straw Yellow

Sommariva Prosecco
di Conegliano-
Valdobbiadene
Superiore Brut

Pale Lemon Yellow

Jacques Lassaigne
Champagne
"Les Vignes de
Montgueux" Blanc
de Blancs Extra Brut

Golden Yellow

Recaredo "Terrers"
Brut Natur Gran
Reserva Corpinatt

Orange/Amber	Light Pink	Dark Pink	Purple
Cà de Noci "Querciole" Frizzante	Ameztoi Getariako Txakolina "Rubentis" Rosado	Renardat Fache Cerdon de Bugey	Bruno Verdi Sangue di Giuda "Vigna Paradiso"

Pét-Nat and the Méthode Ancestrale

How long must a wine trend stick around before it no longer qualifies as such? Whatever the official threshold might be, pét-nat (short for "pétillant-naturel") crossed it long ago. No longer dismissed as a passing fad, the lightly sparkling, often-cloudy style has staked its claim as a fixture of wine's modern mainstream.

As every article ever penned on the subject will tell you, pét-nat owes its cachet to the ancestral method of fermentation (see page 10), an approach that predates the invention of Champagne by more than two centuries—at least in those areas of France where it has historically been practiced. Although the term has no legal definition, it's commonly understood as the oldest and simplest way of getting a wine to sparkle. Unlike Champagne, whose effervescence results from a secondary fermentation through the addition of sugar and yeast, pét-nat derives its fizz from bottling the wine before the primary fermentation has finished, trapping CO_2 and imparting a soft froth of bubbles. In other words, if most sparkling wine production involves coaxing a still wine into sparkling form, pét-nat skips the middle step, allowing carbonation to occur while the juice is still in the process of turning into wine.

Technical details aside, early efforts to pin down the style's history were typically less than helpful. Over the years, articles have dubbed it "Champagne's hip younger sister," "the newest insider sparkling wine," "pre-technological," "a singular experience of terroir," and "sort of accidental, a little dangerous . . . and very much in vogue among the young Californian enorati." Low in alcohol, unfiltered, and often hazy, it's frequently described—for better or worse—as an earthier, funkier, more "honest" or "authentic" style of sparkling wine, which supposedly references some earlier (it's never clear which) period of France's winemaking past.

Confusingly, pét-nat's popular image suggests two contradictory things: on the one hand, it's supposed to be the latest hipster-approved wine trend, and on the other, an old-school throwback steeped in tradition. So what is pét-nat, really?

Though the method might be old, the term *pét-nat* is fairly new, having emerged in France's Loire Valley as recently as the 1990s. During these early days of the natural wine movement, progressive winemakers such as the late Christian Chaussard—widely credited with launching the modern pét-nat movement—were beginning to experiment with a new philosophy of organic viticulture and minimum intervention in the cellar, often with unpredictable results.

As it so happens, pét-nat's genesis (like so many great discoveries) can be ascribed to a happy accident. According to the category's creation myth, the first modern pét-nat came into being when one of Chaussard's demi-sec (or slightly off-dry) whites started to referment in the bottle, resulting in an unintentionally sparkling wine. Rather than dump it and start from scratch, he decided he liked the wine, inadvertent bubbles and all.

The rest is history. Now a fixture of modern wine culture, the globe-trotting style knows no geographical bounds. But if you're looking to get a foothold into the category, there's no better place to start than the early French efforts that first defined it. Though it would be impossible to list them all, here are just a few of the classic Loire examples that have come to embody a canon of their own.

PRODUCERS TO KNOW

Agnès et René Mosse	Le Sot de l'Ange
Domaine Frantz Saumon	Lise & Bertrand Jousset
Domaine Philippe Tessier	Olivier Lemasson
La Grange Tiphaine	Thierry Puzelat (Clos du Tue-Boeuf)
Les Capriades	

The Wine List

Les Capriades "Pet' Sec" Chenin Blanc ($)

Universally hailed as the master of the ancestral method, Pascal Potaire of Les Capriades has dedicated his career to the mission of elevating pét-nat to an artform. Whereas most other producers treat it as a side project, Les Capriades focuses exclusively on the style, and the result of that obsession comes across in pét-nats of uncommon elegance and precision, such as this bone-dry take on chenin blanc that's disgorged for greater transparency.

Agnès et René Mosse "Moussamoussettes" Pétillant Rosé ($)

One of the first pét-nats to register on the US radar, the Mosse "Moussamoussettes" introduced the style to an entire generation of drinkers. Showcasing the best of pét-nat's easygoing side, it's a bright pink, strawberry-scented, ever-so-slightly off-dry blend of grolleau gris and pineau d'aunis, two of the area's obscure indigenous varieties that have gained new relevance thanks to wines like this.

La Grange Tiphaine Montlouis-sur-Loire Brut "Nouveau-Nez" ($)

From the start, the whole point of pét-nat involved breaking the rules. But in 2007, the area of Montlouis approved the creation of an official ancestral-method designation, pétillant originel. Central to that effort, winemaker Damien Delecheneau's contribution to the category epitomizes that seriousness of intent, avoiding the usual goes-down-easy stereotypes in favor of a wine that's every bit as ambitious as the area's celebrated Champagne-method riffs on chenin blanc.

Domaine Philippe Tessier Vin de France "Phil'en Bulle" ($)

Here's another iconic pét-nat from the Loire's grab bag of outré grapes (in this case, the chenin blanc–like romorantin and menu pineau, aka pineau d'aunis), this one hailing from the subregion of Cheverny. Though his approach is entirely natural, Phillippe Tessier's wines never cross the threshold into dangerously funky territory, as his unabashedly delicious "Phil'en Bulle" makes clear. A touch of raw honey finds balance with mouthwatering acidity.

Jean-Pierre Robinot (L'Opéra des Vins) Pétillant-Naturel Rosé "Les Années Folles" ($$)

What better introduction to pét-nat could there be than this hazy, onion peel–colored blend of (primarily) pineau d'Aunis and chenin blanc from Jean-Pierre Robinot, who launched his winemaking career after having operated one of the first natural-wine bars in Paris? Comparatively, this veers toward the contemplative side of style, with a complex earthiness and rosehip-like spice.

The Original Ancestral Wines of France

Pét-Nat's Old-School Precursors

By reintroducing the ancestral method as the hippest thing in wine, pétillant-naturel swiftly went global, giving rise to iterations from Mexico to Maine to Moravia. But like any attempt to revive tradition, when you divorce the technique from the original context, something inevitably gets lost in translation.

Ironically, pét-nat's runaway success as a crown-capped party wine has made it more famous than the original ancestral-method wines that initially inspired it. From the sweet pink fizz of Bugey-Cerdon, tucked in the foothills of the Jura Mountains between Geneva and Lyon, to the ancestral-method wines of southern France's Gaillac, Limoux, and the Rhône's Diois, these storied expressions existed for generations before anyone uttered the words *pét-nat*. But for some reason we hardly ever hear about them.

That paradox is not lost on a winemaker such as Florent Plageoles of Domaine Plageoles, a pioneer of natural winemaking in the southwestern French region of Gaillac. Although he claims not to mind when people label his sparkling Mauzac Nature a pét-nat, he's also quick to highlight the significance of practicing the technique in a place such as Gaillac, where it's deeply embedded within the local heritage. In fact, this tension is inscribed in pét-nat's outlier status within the hierarchy of French wine law. While many ancestral-method wines, including Plageoles's, are guided by local appellation rules, the majority of pét-nat is classified as humble vin de France.

Far from a fun, fizzy side project, Plageoles's goal is to produce a specific style that has been the wine story of Gaillac for generations. Along with their fellow ancestral-method originals, the naturally sparkling wines of Gaillac belong to a unique family that lay claim to a cultural identity of their own. Sadly, the tendency to lump them together under pét-nat's catchall umbrella has prevented a more complex appreciation of what they are.

So what actually differentiates these wines from pét-nat? Well, here's where a little historical knowledge comes in handy. In most places with established ancestral-method traditions (that is, Gaillac, Limoux, and the like), the technique was a simple by-product of the seasons. Fermentation would continue until the onset of winter, when the cold would put the wine to sleep. Come spring, the warm weather would fire up the fermentation again, creating a naturally bubbly wine.

Most of France's original ancestral-method wines now undergo a technological approximation of this process through refrigeration and filtration, artificially halting the fermentation in tank. After a period of time, the half-fermented juice is then bottled and the fermentation resumes. Pét-nat, on the other hand, almost always goes straight from tank to bottle—an uninterrupted continuation of the primary fermentation. Technical distinctions come into play as well, particularly concerning disgorgement. Unlike many pét-nats, which are often (though not always) bottled with the deposit of sediment intact, most canonical ancestral-method wines are disgorged in the interest of creating a cleaner commercial product.

That seriousness of intent applies to the revered Renardat-Fâche estate, one of the most conscientious stewards of Bugey's heritage. Now in its eighth generation of family leadership under winemaker Élie Renardat-Fâche, the winery produces just one sparkling wine for commercial release: its iconic Cerdon du Bugey. Over the years, the family has perfected a rigorous approach to the ancestral method that—in stark contrast to much pét-nat—leaves little to chance. This involves deliberately chilling the wine in the tank to halt the primary fermentation, then lightly filtering before bottling and storing the wine at cold temperatures to preserve delicacy and freshness. Berryish, mineral-driven, and just the right amount of sweet, it possesses the same alpine purity that has revived interest in Savoie's wines as a whole.

Granted, pét-nat's popularity initially paved the way for the wider appreciation of wines such as these and countless others. But the time has come to meet them on their own terms. At a moment when so much modern wine culture trades on a connection to the past, real or imagined, they serve as a potent reminder that sometimes the most enduring traditions are those we never even knew we've ignored.

PRODUCERS TO KNOW

David Bautin	Domaine Plageoles
Domaine Achard-Vincent	Domaine Renardat-Fâche
Domaine Les Hautes Terres	Monge Granon
Domaine Martinolles	Patrick Bottex

The Wine List

Domaine Renardat-Fâche Cerdon du Bugey ($)

Once described by wine writer Jon Bonné as "the happiest wine in the world," Renardat-Fâche's example is arguably the standard bearer for the sparkling wines of Bugey. Bottled without the lees, it pours a transparent strawberry pink, all the better to highlight its crystalline "mountain air" freshness and succulent red fruit that its ample sugar content only intensifies.

Domaine Plageoles Mauzac Nature ($)

Exemplifying the natural wine movement's "what's old is new" mantra, the acclaimed Plageoles estate is among just a handful of winemakers in the Gaillac region keeping the area's ancestral-method traditions alive. Hazy and floral with a twinge of orange blossom and apricot, its sparkling mauzac is as OG as it gets, with a light froth of bubbles and a whiff of cider-like funk.

David Bautin Clairette de Die "Tradition" ($)

An oasis of fizzy whites in a part of France known for its burly reds, the Rhône Valley's Diois region specializes in clairette de Die, another semisweet, sparkling dessert wine based off of clairette and muscat grapes. Gently sweet with a hint of lemon curd and a cleansing rinse of acidity, this one, from independent grower David Bautin, drinks like the wine equivalent of Key lime pie.

Italy

Franciacorta and the Metodo Classico Wines of the North

Fantasize for a moment that you're a member of Milan's well-heeled elite—perhaps the founder of a major design studio or a titan of the textile industry. It goes without saying that you'd drink plenty of Champagne. (Italy imports more than eight million bottles per year, most of it destined for the wealthy northern capital.) But when you weren't drinking Champagne, you'd be drinking Franciacorta, long considered the local equivalent.

Produced in the Lombardy region's Brescia Province near the resort-studded shores of Lake Iseo, just over an hour's drive (or under, if you drive like an Italian) east of Milan, the spumante (Italian for "fully sparkling") wines of Franciacorta represent Italian fizz at its most ambitious. Developed during the 1960s and 1970s, the category sought to fill a gap in the Italian market for high-end bubbly by attempting to rival Champagne. Using the Champagne method (here called the metodo classico) meant adopting the classic Champenois grapes of pinot noir and chardonnay (plus a smidgen of pinot blanc) and, all too often, emulating Champagne's luxury branding as well.

Within Italy, Franciacorta has achieved enormous success. Popping a bottle during the aperitivo hour as an alternative to Champagne has become an act of national pride. But if Franciacorta has struggled to catch on in the United States, that comparison is largely to blame. Unfortunately, Champagne-like aspirations come with prices to match, making it difficult to convince the average consumer to shell out for an obscure substitute when they could just as easily buy the real thing.

Faced with this identity crisis, a growing number of Franciacorta producers have started to doubt the founding logic that brought Franciacorta into existence. Though few and far between, they're laying the foundations for a new generation of estate-grown and -bottled sparkling wines that seek to answer an existential question: What would it mean to make an authentically Italian style of Franciacorta—one that made no attempt at imitation but instead telegraphed its own innate "Franciacorta-ness," as it were?

The New Franciacorta

Reimagining Franciacorta as a wine of terroir is no easy task. In effect, it requires a complete rethinking of the area and its wines from the ground up—literally. Even from the most basic perspective of geography and climate, the Champagne analogy never made much sense. Despite being located in the foothills of the Alps, Franciacorta is considerably warmer, lending its grapes a natural predisposition toward ripeness that marginal Champagne notoriously lacks. As a general rule, Franciacorta tends to be rounder, fleshier, and more fruit-forward: think full-bodied Italian swagger more than buttoned-up Champagne formality. Fittingly, rather than fashioning their wines into a ready-made mold based on the latter, the winemakers advancing the region's evolution are embracing Franciacorta's natural endowments in several critical ways, both in the vineyard and in the cellar.

In addition to facilitating chemical-free farming (Franciacorta is one of Italy's leading regions for organic viticulture), the area's ability to yield perfectly ripe grapes has empowered terroir-minded winemakers to drastically reduce the levels of dosage in their wines, ushering in a wave of dosaggio zero bottlings. Early proponents of this alternative mind-set, Giovanni Arcari and Nico Danesi of the pioneering Arcari e Danesi project continue to be the movement's standard-bearers, but they've been joined by like-minded peers, including the Cà del Vént winery, in the hills of Campiani di Cellatica, and Divella Gussago, the brainchild of rising star Alessandra Divella, among others.

In their collective effort to cast off Champagne's influence, it might sound like Franciacorta's new guard has merely replaced one model of that region with another, borrowing from the grower Champagne move-ment's bag of tricks. But at a time when so many sparkling wine regions across the globe have adopted the same approach, using bubbles as a medium for terroir, the grower approach now applies so much more broadly. What matters is the end result, and on that front there's no denying that the sparkling wines defining Franciacorta's next chapter rank among the most exciting and original found in the market today.

PRODUCERS TO KNOW

Arcari + Danesi	Nicola Gatta
Cà del Vént	Ravarini
Casa Caterina	1707 Franciacorta
Divella Gussago	Solo Uva
Il Pendio	

Satèn Franciacorta

For the most part, Franciacorta has borrowed Champagne's familiar nomenclature and classification system to delineate its range of styles. These include blanc de blancs (made only from chardonnay and pinot blanc), blanc de noirs (100 percent pinot noir), and rosé (at least 25 percent pinot noir in the base wine) and range from basic nonvintage blends to millesimato (or vintage-dated) versions. There's also a riserva designation requiring a minimum of sixty months aging on the lees, which roughly corresponds to the tête de cuvée (prestige) bottlings of major Champagne houses. If you spend enough time exploring Franciacorta, however, you'll start noticing certain bottles that bear the label "Satèn." Adapted from "silken" in Italian (a nod to the area's historic silk industry), the term refers to a more softly sparkling style of Franciacorta, bottled with less pressure and made from 100 percent chardonnay.

The Other Metodo Classico Wines of the Italian Alps

As the Franciacorta revolution unfolds, the region is emerging as the most visible focal point of a wider renaissance of metodo classico winemaking that has taken hold across the top of the boot. Notably, the mountain region of Trentino, which spans the lower half of the Adige Valley and is surrounded by the snowcapped peaks of the Dolomites, has been a source of Champagne-method sparkling wines since 1902, when the area's largest firm, Ferrari (no relation to the sportscar), set up shop there. Utilizing the same grapes (pinot noir, pinot blanc, and chardonnay) with the addition of pinot meunier, the sparklers made under the Trentodoc designation shared Franciacorta's early attempts to imitate Champagne. At their best, they express themselves via a starker, more streamlined alpine style.

Though big brands, like Ferrari and Rotari, continue to dominate the area, card-carrying naturalist Matteo Furlani of Trento's Cantina Furlani represents a noteworthy exception to the local status quo. Along with a handful of frizzante (Italian for "lightly sparkling") ancestral-method wines from native grapes such as nosiola and teroldego, he makes two mind-bending "brut natur" bottlings—one white, one rosé—from pinot noir and chardonnay according to what he describes as the metodo interrotto, or "interrupted method": namely, the classical Champagne method minus the final step of disgorgement, resulting in a cloudy wine that defies expectations.

Far more famous as the birthplace of Barolo and Barbaresco—arguably Italy's greatest, age-worthiest reds—the Piedmont region's Langhe area has lately been turning out teensy quantities of metodo classico fizz under the Alta Langa banner, again from pinot noir and chardonnay. Barolo producer Enrico Serafino's versions are among the best known. For sparkling wines with a more indigenously Piedmontese feel, look for niche expressions such as cult producer Luigi Ferrando's Erbaluce di Caluso Spumante "Pas Dosè," made from the obscure erbaluce grape (a specialty of his subzone of Caluso), or Castello di Verduno's "S-ciopét," a rose petal–scented rosé interpretation of the pelaverga piccolo variety (yet another of Piedmont's idiosyncratic bit players).

The Wine List

Arcari + Danesi Franciacorta "Dosaggio Zero" ($$)

This is the kind of grower of Franciacorta that shows the region at its purest and most authentically northern Italian. Committed to establishing Franciacorta's identity on its own terms, Giovanni Arcari and Nico Danesi led the movement of zéro dosage in Franciacorta—an approach that allows the wine's underlying richness and stone-fruit qualities to assume center stage.

Cà del Vént "Memoria" Spumante Brut Pas Operé ($$$)

Yes, this is a bit of a splurge (albeit a reasonable one compared to what you'd expect to shell out for Champagne of comparable quality), but Antonio Tornincasa is making some of Italy's purest and most site-expressive metodo classico wines under his Cà del Vént label. Refermented in bottle using grape must of the same vintage and bottled without dosage, his "Memoria"—a blend of mostly chardonnay with a splash of pinot noir—feels clawed from the chalky soils of Campiani di Cellatica, a subzone known for producing Franciacorta's most elegant wines.

Divella Gussago Dosaggio Zero Blanc de Blancs ($$)

While still in her twenties, self-taught winemaker Alessandra Divella arrived in the province of Gussago in the eastern sector of Franciacorta with a mission: to produce pristine, place-driven metodo classico bubbles that apply a "grower" approach to the two small plots of organically farmed vines she rents from a local family. Her entry-level blanc de blancs is a tour de force, combining layers of orchard fruit with a fine persistent bead of bubbles and a lightly etched minerality.

Ferrando Erbaluce di Caluso Spumante "La Torrazza" ($$)

It's Ferrando's cult reds, grown high in the foothills of the northernmost corner of Piedmont, that most often pop up in bottle shots on sommelier Instagram feeds. Those in the know also wax poetic over the winery's erbaluce, the obscure local white of the Caluso zone. Straw-colored and honeyed, this weird yet wonderful metodo classico version spends up to thirty-six months on the lees, lending it a toasty marzipan quality.

Cantina Furlani Brut Natur "Metodo Interrotto" ($$)

In an area dominated by commercial sparkling wine houses turning out safe, by-the-numbers spumante, Trento's Matteo Furlani has carved his own radical path to cult stardom. Bottled under crown cap and without disgorging, his brut natur "Metodo Interrotto" drinks like a "fun-house mirror" version of Trentodoc, raw and unfiltered.

The Prosecco Story

Italy produces more wine per year than any other country on Earth, including its great rival France. This distinction is owed in no small part to the oceans of commercial Prosecco that flow into the market annually. In 2013, after several years of record-breaking sales, Prosecco surpassed Champagne as the bestselling sparkling wine in the world (by volume, if not by price), and the area hasn't looked back since.

If you're surprised to hear Prosecco referred to as a region rather than a style, you're not alone. Universally considered a generic or "default" form of fizz, it's poured indiscriminately at bridal showers and gallery openings and bottomless brunches—pretty much anywhere bubbles play a purely perfunctory role.

By now, Prosecco's ubiquity as a product has all but blotted out its identity as a place. But let's not begrudge Prosecco its commercial success or, for that matter, its lack of fine-wine ambition. The whole point of Prosecco is that it's categorically *not* Champagne. You can throw it into a spritz without any guilt, or you can guzzle it on its own. Above all, it encapsulates the spirit of la dolce vita, the Italian art of everyday living: a sunset drink on the terrace of a Venetian café— or somewhat less romantically, in a cramped Brooklyn backyard.

Stylistically, this easy-drinking appeal is the direct result of the specific way Prosecco is made. Held up as the definitive example of the Charmat (or tank-fermented) method of sparkling wine production (see page 8), Prosecco is at its best when it openly embraces the qualities associated with the technique. In addition to preserving the fresh primary aromas of glera, Prosecco's signature grape—think honeysuckle and peach versus Champagne's yeast-driven complexity—Charmat lends itself to lighter, fruitier wines with gentler bubbles meant to be popped as soon as possible.

That commercial formula turned Prosecco into the mass-market phenomenon it is today. Over the years, as demand continued to soar, production swelled to keep up. As a result, the region lobbied to expand its official boundaries beyond its historic center of production. The official Prosecco zone now encompasses a vast expanse of land, extending across nine different provinces from the original Veneto area east to Friuli, all the better to crank out enormous quantities of bubbly on a global scale.

As the Prosecco boom shows no signs of relenting, the region's future hinges on a crucial question: Will "brand Prosecco" reign supreme, or is there another way forward—one that, ideally, reintroduces drinkers to Prosecco as a wine of place?

Conegliano and Valdobbiadene: Prosecco's OG Home

If Prosecco can return to being a wine of place, it would be in the bucolic vineyards that unfurl between the hilltop villages of Conegliano and Valdobbiadene, Prosecco's historical home. Encompassing what's now known as the Prosecco Superiore zone, fifty miles or so north of Venice, the area presents a welcome contrast to the gigantic corporate wineries that source their grapes by the truckload from the flat Treviso plains.

Harvested from the same steep, largely family-owned sites that the area's growers have tended for centuries, the top Prosecco Superiore bottles that bear the Conegliano and Valdobbiadene names on their label taste like Prosecco was meant to taste: simple, perhaps—at least, compared to the savory, mature aromas of Champagne-method wines—but in all the right ways, with crisp minerality, bright bubbles, and, in lieu of synthetic fruit flavors, loads of ripe apple and pear. Sure, you can expect to pay slightly more for carefully crafted bottles from smaller producers, such as Le Vigne di Alice or Sommariva (think closer to twenty dollars per bottle, rather than ten or twelve dollars), but that's a small premium for wine that tastes like it comes from an actual "somewhere."

Cartizze: Prosecco's "Grand Cru"

In 2009, Prosecco producers within the classic Prosecco Superiore zone of Conegliano-Valdobbiadene received the right to label their wines with the names of forty-three specific villages or microzones known as "Rives." While designations such as Rive di Manzana, for instance, or Rive di Guia might not mean much to consumers, the objective behind the initiative deserves praise: to further define the terroirs of Prosecco and shift the conversation back to the land itself.

Realistically, it's probably a stretch to imagine the average Prosecco drinker studying up on the subtle distinctions among different villages and soil types. For now, if you do encounter a bottle that lists one of the official Rives, you can at least take it as a sign that someone cares.

Of all the Superiore subzones, one particular hillside has always stood out from the rest, signifying the apex of quality within this site-specific Prosecco paradigm. In the heart of Valdobbiadene, near the parish of San Pietro di Barbozza, the steep slope of Cartizze has been celebrated for generations as the source of Prosecco's finest wines.

Because of Cartizze's ability to coax grapes to luxurious levels of ripeness, it offers up the most opulent and concentrated expression of Prosecco—adjectives not typically associated with the category. Are they worth it? Like anything, that depends. Top examples can easily fetch upward of forty dollars—a price point that's sure to trigger more than a little cognitive dissonance among drinkers accustomed to thinking of Prosecco as something you pour into your mimosa. Furthermore, the historic tendency toward semisweet styles (confusingly labeled "dry" or "extra dry") runs counter to contemporary taste.

Still, in the hands of the right producer, such as Col Vetoraz or Ruggero Ruggeri's Ruge project, Cartizze offers up what might be considered a spiritual apotheosis of Prosecco, full of richness and ripe orchard fruit but without sacrificing the "immediate gratification" factor that made Prosecco a breakout hit in the first place.

The Rebirth of Col Fondo

If the Rive movement represents one front in the fight against boring, industrial Prosecco, that revolution assumes its most radical form in a throwback style known as col fondo. Meaning "with its bottom," or "with sediment," the term refers to an unfiltered, notably cloudy style of Prosecco, fermented not in the massive stainless-steel tanks that dominate today but directly in bottle with the deposit of dead yeast cells intact. You'll also see it labeled as sui lieviti (on the lees) or rifermentato in bottiglia (refermented in bottle).

This drier, yeastier, and less aggressively sparkling (or frizzante) version of the wine bears little resemblance to the conventional stuff we all know so well, but it has been produced in the hills of Conegliano-Valdobbiadene for longer than anyone can remember. Although many producers abandoned col fondo in the 1970s, when Prosecco transformed itself into a brand, lately the style has been bubbling up again, a specialty of the small family growers that have tended their vines for generations. And at a time when the wine world has reveled in the reclamation of ancient styles, col fondo checks off all the right boxes; to many, the movement is responsible for Prosecco's best wines.

While some Italian col fondo is produced like pét-nat, as the result of one fermentation, the technical details have evolved over time. Many producers of natural Prosecco now use the term *metodo ancestrale* to refer to wines that represent something of a rural halfway house between the ancestral and Champagne methods, in which natural grape must is added to a still base wine before bottling. The final impression conjures the rustic fizz of ages gone by, even if the technique has been updated.

It's tempting to view the col fondo movement as the latest wave in a wider ripple of funky, cloudy fizz. For many col fondistas, however, the style's revival transcends mere fashion. In its thirst-quenching simplicity and rawness, it offers a vehicle for telling the story of the land of their forebears and, in the process, imbuing Prosecco with a newfound relevance.

PRODUCERS TO KNOW

Adriano Adami	Costadilà
Bele Casel	Le Vigne di Alice
Bisol	Ruge
Bisson	Sommariva
Ca' dei Zago	Sorelle Bronca
Casa Belfi	Zanotto
Casa Coste Piane	

The Wine List

Sommariva Prosecco di Conegliano-Valdobbiadene Superiore Brut ($)

If you're going to drink fifteen-dollar Prosecco, why not drink this one, produced by actual people—the Sommariva family has been farming the area's vines for ages—in the historic hills of the Prosecco Superiore zone. Clean, fresh, and fruit-driven, it's what Prosecco was always meant to be.

Bisson Marca Trevigiana Glera Frizzante ($)

It's odd that Pierluigi Lugano, the winemaking legend of the coastal Liguria region, also produces one of the iconic wines of Prosecco, nearly three hundred miles away. Produced in collaboration with Eli Spagnol of the Torre Zecchei winery in the heart of Valdobbiadene, it's among the most reliable values in sparkling wine and a tried-and-true "by-the-glass" sommelier favorite.

Le Vigne di Alice Prosecco "A Fondo" NV ($)

Paying homage to the cloudy, bottle-fermented wines that her grandfather Angelo made during her childhood, winemaker Cinzia Canzian's piercing, bone-dry col fondo offers a glimpse of Prosecco's future by way of the past. Sourced from organically farmed grapes, it has salty minerality and a slight creaminess coming from the presence of the lees.

Casa Coste Piane Prosecco di Valdobbiadene Sur Lie ($)

One of the first examples of the unfiltered, bottle-fermented col fondo style to gain Stateside attention, Casa Coste Piane's version remains a benchmark of the category. Lightly silted and aromatically bright, it's a defining emblem of col fondo's "back to the basics" philosophy.

Emilia-Romagna

The Land of Lambrusco (and Beyond)

The first thing you're likely to learn about Lambrusco, the famous sparkling red of Italy's Emilia-Romagna region, is that its name refers to both the wine itself and the family of grapes from which the wine is made. The second thing you'll learn is how much of it you'd be wise to avoid.

Ever since the 1970s and 1980s, when an invasion of sweet, mass-market brands such as Riunite transformed Lambrusco into the era's bestselling imported wine, the story of this Emilia-Romagna native has centered on its lowbrow image. But during the last two decades, not only has Lambrusco reclaimed its reputation as one of the world's singular sparkling wines, but Emilia-Romagna has shown that its prowess with bubbly goes well beyond Lambrusco. From its Adriatic coastline to the rolling foothills outside Lombardy, the area is now defined by sparkling expressions from a dizzying array of grapes and growing regions.

This "new" wave of Emilia-Romagna sparklers isn't new at all, but a return to the old-school style of frizzante wines that were once more widespread regional staples. Like their col fondo equivalents in Prosecco, these gently sparkling wines derive their bubbles naturally, through the time-honored method of refermentation in bottle (rifermentato in bottiglia).

On the surface, the Italian category shares all the chuggable, thirst-quenching qualities that transformed pét-nat into an overnight sensation—except that its history in the area stretches back centuries. Originally designed for local consumption, the rifermentato in bottiglia style fueled a thriving cottage industry for generations that nearly vanished after the shift to industrial winemaking in Italy's postwar economic boom.

Much of the bubbly from Emilia-Romagna, up through Veneto's Prosecco country, started being produced at scale using the Charmat method. It wasn't until the 1990s and early aughts that a small cadre of producers, including natural-wine luminaries Vittorio Graziano, Camillo Donati, and Luciano and Sara Saetti, actively sought to revive the rifermentato in bottiglia approach.

This shift reopened a window into the past that decades of chemical-dependent agriculture and bulk production had all but obliterated. The Lambrusco that has come out of this revival has reimagined it as a multifaceted wine of place, allowing drinkers to pick apart the nuances among the various strains of grapes and the growing areas they call home. These include the strawberry-hued Lambrusco di Sorbara, grown to the north of Modena (and giving the lightest wines), and the darker, more tannic examples from Lambrusco Grasparossa di Castelvetro to the south. Lambrusco Salamino di Santa Croce falls somewhere between the two, combining the floral delicacy of the Sorbara grape with the richness and structure of its grasparossa kin.

Beyond Lambrusco

The reclamation of "real" Lambrusco would be enough to push Emilia-Romagna back into the spotlight but there's much more to the region's story. Many of the producers who are responsible for Lambrusco's artisanal revival are also endeavoring to paint a more-detailed portrait of the classic Lambrusco areas of Parma, Modena, and Reggio Emilia. Consider Giovanni and Alberto Masini of the Cà de Noci estate, stewards of vanishing grapes such as spergola, sgavetta, and malbo gentile, which yield both still and sparkling wines. Or a luminary such as Camillo Donati, who's helped establish a new benchmark with his bottle-fermented Lambrusco, while also exploring bottle-fermented, skin-contact render-ings of the trebbiano and malvasia di candia grapes. Each offers proof that the area never had just one thing to say.

Beyond Lambrusco's historic home turf, other lesser-known parts of Emilia-Romagna have also stepped forward of late, clawing their way out of obscurity thanks to the wider vogue for naturally sparkling wines. In particular, the remote Colli Piacentini area—a steep, hilly swath of vineyards in the region's extreme northwest corner—has become an increasingly sought-after hot zone for alternative winemaking.

Much of the buzz that the area has generated has centered around an experimental uprising of skin-contact whites from cult producers such as La Stoppa and Denavolo. However, Bulli's frizzante represents a tradition as old as the Piacenza hills themselves. Along with rising stars such as minimal interventionist Massimiliano Croci, Bulli is highlighting the area's distinct blend of native grapes, including barbera, croatina, uva rara, malvasia, and the lesser-known ortrugo. Collectively, the area offers its own subgenre of Emilia-Romagna frizzante, which arguably has more in common with the sparkling wines of Lombardy's Oltrepò Pavese, just a short drive away, than with the Lambrusco strongholds of the central flatlands outside Modena.

Down along the Adriatic, in the sleepy seaside area of Bosco Eliceo, Mirco Mariotti is crafting some of the region's most idiosyncratic sparklers. Together, they represent a completely different—and until now virtually unknown—side of the region. His tangy, frothy "Sèt e Mèz" rosé, for instance, is composed of the virtually unknown fortana grape, which he sources from one-hundred-year-old vines planted in beach sand roughly three hundred yards from the sea. It's got a subtle spice and strawberry brightness reminiscent of Jura poulsard, but with the same pungent, salt-tinged mineral bite found across so many of the wines up and down Italy's Adriatic coastline. Equally noteworthy is his "Smarazen," a gently sparkling white sourced from eighty-year-old trebbiano romagnolo and malvasia di candia vines planted in the same sandy soils. Like all of the wines that best represent Emilia-Romagna, Mariotti's work presents a fundamental paradox of modern wine culture, pointing out how the taste of the past is also the taste of today.

PRODUCERS TO KNOW

Bulli	Denny Bini (Podere Cipolla)
Cà de Noci	Mirco Mariotti
Camillo Donati	Vigneto Saetti
Cinque Campi	Vittorio Graziano
Croci	

The Wine List

Cinque Campi Lambrusco Rosso ($)

A classic take on lambrusco grasparossa (with a smattering of malbo gentile and marzemino), this undisgorged, unsulfured frizzante showcases the fleshy, dark-fruited depth that is the strain's signature. Generously fizzy with a mouthful of blackberry, violet, and damp earth, it's custom-built to drink with hearty fare.

Bulli Sampagnino Colli Piacentini Frizzante ($)

In addition to a fizzy red from barbera and bonarda, Leonard Bulli produces two bottle-fermented whites: one focusing exclusively on ortrugo, a grape traditionally incorporated into blends, and this kitchen-sink mix of local varieties, including uva sampagnina (aka marsanne), moscato giallo, and malvasia di candia, plus extreme rarities such as bervedino and verdea. Yellow-fruited and salty with an herbal edge, it's the sort of old-school frizzante once found only in the family-run trattorias of the Colli Piacentini.

Cà de Noci "Querciole" Frizzante ($)

Once widespread in Reggio Emilia, the resurrection of the spergola grape in bottles such as the Masini brothers' "Querciole," which undergoes three days of skin contact, yields a bright yet savory, almost musky aspect with a smack of tannin and aromas of chamomile tea.

Lambrusco Camillo Donati Lambrusco dell'Emilia ($)

Leave it to one of the founding fathers of Emilia-Romagna's natural-wine scene to deliver what may very well be the platonic ideal of old-school, bottle-fermented Lambrusco. Epitomizing all that's lovable about the style, it delivers a one-two punch of blackberry and black licorice.

Mirco Mariotti "Sèt e Mèz" Fortana dell'Emilia Rosato ($)

You could ask for no greater testament to Emilia-Romagna's current diversity than Mirco Mariotti's fortana-based frizzante rosé, a wine that speaks more of the salty Adriatic coastline than the fertile plains around Modena. The fact that you can get this much depth and character out of a sub-twenty-dollar bottle is nothing short of a modern miracle.

Croci Gutturnio DOC Frizzante Rosso ($)

Part of the minimal-intervention cohort that is quietly remaking the Colli Piacentini into a hotbed of naturalist activity, Massimiliano Croci produces only three wines, all of them cloudy and fermented in bottle. His only bubbly red, this classic blend of barbera and croatina from the sandy soils of the Gutturnio DOC goes down easy, with a sour-cherry edge and a touch of funk.

The Other Bubbly Wines of Italy

If Prosecco fatigue has you down, here's the good news. From the top of the boot down to the sole, there's not a region in Italy where sparkling wine of some kind or another isn't being made. Of course, this being Italy—a republic that essentially consisted of a disparate patchwork of feuding kingdoms and nation-states until Garibaldi united them under one rule in 1861—the task of imposing order upon this glorious mess of regional expressions is anything but obvious. In lieu of a comprehensive overview, the most viable solution is to sketch out some of the major fizzy highlights and pockets of interest that exist outside the "main attractions" for which Italian bubbly is best known.

The Frizzante Wines of Piedmont and Lombardy

Piedmont is best known as the home of heavy-hitting Barolo and Barbaresco, Italian wine's crowning achievements.

But every great wine region also needs its form of comic relief. In Piedmont, that role has traditionally fallen to the area's deep (and deeply commercial) history of semisweet sparkling wine production. Throughout much of the twentieth century, cheap, industrial Asti Spumante from supermarket brands typified that tradition. Based upon the highly aromatic moscato bianco grape, the simple, tank-fermented Asti Spumante style (that is, spumante, or "fully sparkling," wine from the area of Asti) is perhaps best understood as the disco-era equivalent of the modern Prosecco craze.

Beyond this mass-market image, however, Piedmont's roster of sugar-kissed sparkling wines deserves a place in the modern repertoire. It's just a question of knowing where to look. Notably, Asti Spumante's sweeter, frizzante (softly sparkling) cousin, Moscato d'Asti, embodies a platonic ideal for this style of the grape. Floral (think jasmine and honeysuckle) with flavors of candied lemon, powdered sugar, and apricot, it's also lower in alcohol (typically just 5.5 percent alcohol by volume), making it right for nearly any occasion. Many of the top examples come from several benchmark Barolo producers behind Piedmont's top reds (look for Vietti, Barale Fratelli, De Forville, and Oddero, among others).

In the same sweet and fizzy family, there's also Brachetto d'Acqui, essentially Moscato d'Asti's dark pink equivalent, with its wild-berry bramble and fresh floral aromas. And finally, heading east from Piedmont into the foothills of Lombardy, the Oltrepò Pavese region south of Milan produces some singular frizzante of its own, including Sangue di Giuda (meaning "Blood of Judas"), another versatile semisweet red made from a blend of four indigenous grapes: croatina, uvra rara, vespolina, and barbera. Though further research is needed, the local friars once believed it to be an aphrodisiac. The Bruno Verdi winery, now run by the winemaker's son, Paolo, produces the definitive example.

PRODUCERS TO KNOW

Barale Fratelli	Elio Perrone
Braida di Giacomo Bologna	Oddero
Bruno Verdi	Paolo Pizzorni
De Forville	Vietti

The Metodo Classico Upstarts of Sicily and Campania

A modern mecca for cool-hunting Italian-wine lovers, Sicily has catapulted itself from a rustic source of bulk reds to the beating heart of Italy's new avant-garde. Admittedly, still wines continue to generate most of that attention, but a mini-resurgence of traditional-method Sicilian sparklers testifies to the island's modern spirit of experimentation.

Nowhere is that vision on greater display than thousands of feet up in the air on the slopes of Mount Etna, Europe's tallest active volcano. The area first attracted attention for mineral, savory reds made from the nerello mascalese and nerello cappuccio grapes, but the same high-elevation freshness and smoky minerality finds its way into some of Italy's most distinctive sparkling wines. Additionally, in the up-and-coming Vittoria area, natural-wine pioneer Giusto Occhipinti's COS winery channels the cult frappato grape into a bracing metodo classico bottled with zero dosage, while on Sicily's extreme western coast, young winemaker Alessandro Viola is incorporating grillo, inzolia, and cataratto—the classic varieties of Marsala, the area's famous fortified wine—into cutting-edge whites, including his sparkling Blanc de Blancs Pas Dosé.

Sharing similar southern spirit, the Campania region in the shadows of Mount Vesuvius has long specialized in sparkling red Gragnano, the sweetish, easy-drinking staple of the pizza parlors of Naples. More recently, though, next-gen producers such as Ciro Picariello and De Conciliis have started making Champagne-method wines from local grapes such as fiano (the noble white of the Italian south) and aglianico (its red counterpart) that drink like liquid facsimiles of the area's ashy volcanic soils.

PRODUCERS TO KNOW

Alessandro Viola	De Conciliis
Ciro Picariello	Murgo
COS	Salvo Foti

The Italian Pét-Nat Diaspora

Beyond col fondo Prosecco and the bottle-fermented frizzante wines of Emilia-Romagna—which despite certain aesthetic similarities comprise a category of their own—Italy has cultivated a pretty impressive pét-nat game. That's unsurprising given the country boasts one of the world's most advanced natural-wine scenes, second only to that of France. The style's popularity has brought bubbles to just about every corner of the boot, including many that historically lacked sparkling wine traditions. Even in an area as established as Tuscany—the land of red Chianti and Brunello di Montalcino—rebels such as Silvio Messana (of the Montesecondo winery) and Margherita and Francesca Padovani of Montalcino's Fonterenza estate have tried their hands at the style.

PRODUCERS TO KNOW

Ancarini	La Staffa
Angiolino Maule	Ribelà
Bera Vittorio e Figli	Silvio Messana
Colombaia	Tenuta Ca' Sciampagne
Fonterenza	Tiberi
Francesco Cirelli	Valli Unite
Furlani	

The Wine List

Oddero Moscato d'Asti ($)

The polar opposite of its structured, age-worthy Barolo and Barbaresco, Oddero's sugary (but never saccharine), softly frizzante Moscato d'Asti makes no demands other than to be enjoyed. Simply put, this is instant gratification in a bottle, all honeysuckle and candied peach.

Bruno Verdi Sangue di Giuda "Paradiso" ($)

For decades, the Verdi family has bestowed upon the world the definitive example of Sangue di Giuda, one of Italy's least-known but most intriguing sparkling reds. From the Paradiso vineyard in the heart of Lombardy's Oltrepò Pavese, it's bottled at just 7.5 percent alcohol and reveals a perfect balance among candied-cherry sweetness, soft effervescence, and a grippy texture that's designed to cut right through a plate of the area's famous salami.

Alessandro Viola Blanc de Blancs Pas Dosé Metodo Classico ($$)

Historically renowned for the fortified wine that bears its name (and its namesake chicken dish), the Sicilian area of Marsala has recently made waves for its next-gen dry whites from the grillo, inzolia, and catarratto grapes. At the vanguard of that transformation, winemaker Alessandro Viola is the genius behind this metodo classico take on catarratto, which tastes like the distilled essence of Sicily: think pine resin, yellow plum, and basil.

Silvio Messana Ghazii Pét-Nat Rosato ($)

A pioneer of natural wine in Tuscany's conservative Chianti Classico area, Silvio Messana's sangiovese-based wines—sourced from the biodynamic vineyards of his Montesecondo estate—have become catnip for wine geeks. He made the first vintage of this watermelon-hued pét-nat in 2018, which showcases sangiovese's signature drinkability in an entirely unexpected format.

Bera Vittorio e Figli "Arcese" ($)

One of the more idiosyncratic frizzante wines to emerge from the classic region of Piedmont, the dry "Arcese" bottling from Bera Vittorio e Figli— among the area's finest moscato producers—derives its name from a portmanteau of the arneis and cortese grapes, though some vermentino and sauvignon blanc are in the mix as well. High-toned and wildly floral, it's bottled unfiltered with a touch of residual sugar, resulting in a natural prickle of CO_2.

Ciro Picariello Brut Contadino ($$)

When Campania's star white grape, fiano, gets the metodo classico treatment, the technique amplifies the variety's signature fleshy texture and smoky salinity. This full-bodied version from the celebrated Ciro Picariello estate, the source of some of the area's finest dry whites, has all the makings—nutty, ashy edged, and herbal—of a new classic of the Italian south.

Sparkling Wine Cocktails

Aperol Spritz

The spritz construct of sparkling wine, bitter liqueur, and bubbly water is incredibly versatile. But Aperol, the sunset-colored Italian bitter liqueur from Padua, is the classic, providing the lightly sweet base for this afternoon cooler.

1 ounce Aperol

2 ounces sparkling wine, preferably dry Prosecco

1 ounce soda water

Garnish: Orange or lemon slice (or both)

Add Aperol, sparkling wine, and soda water to a Collins or wine glass. Add ice and stir gently. Garnish with an orange or lemon slice.

Death in the Afternoon

Bizarrely, Ernest Hemingway extended the gravitas of *Death in the Afternoon*, the title of his 1932 novel about the denouement of bullfighting in Spain, to this minimalist cocktail that's nothing more than Champagne with a shot of absinthe. The recipe ran in a celebrity drinks book in 1932. The seriousness with which Hemingway approached his cocktail was evidenced by his recipe instructions: to drink three to five of these at a time.

¼-½ ounce absinthe

1 dash simple syrup (1:1 sugar water; optional)

Champagne or dry sparkling wine, to top

Add absinthe and simple syrup (if using) to a flute. Slowly top with chilled Champagne or sparkling wine.

French 75

History says that this Champagne cocktail originated at Harry's New York Bar, in Paris, in the early 1900s, but it was co-opted and made legendary shortly thereafter by Arnaud's French 75 bar in New Orleans. The original recipe calls for Cognac combined with Champagne, lemon juice, and sugar, but somewhere along the line, it became fashionable to make the drink with gin instead. The Cognac gives the cocktail more depth and a little bit of spice, making it a great bubbly drink for the fall and winter. The livelier gin version (a gin sour royale, really) is best in warm weather.

2 ounces cognac or gin

½ ounce lemon juice

¼ ounce simple syrup
(1:1 sugar:water)

3 ounces Champagne or
dry sparkling wine

Garnish: Long, curly lemon peel

Add Cognac, lemon juice, and simple syrup to a cocktail shaker. Add ice and shake until chilled. Strain into a coupe or a flute and top with Champagne or sparkling wine. Garnish with a long, curly lemon peel.

Negroni Sbagliato

This twist on the Negroni allegedly came to be when a Milanese bartender reached for a bottle of Prosecco rather than gin when making the classic drink—the sbagliato addendum translates to mean "incorrect" or "mistaken." But, in fact, the buoyantly bitter Italian aperitivo drink is anything but incorrect. If the sbagliato is wrong, you don't want to be right.

1 ounce Campari

1 ounce sweet vermouth

3 ounces Prosecco
(or any dry sparkling wine), to top

Garnish: Orange peel

In a rocks or lowball glass, add Campari, sweet vermouth, and ice. Top with Prosecco and stir gently to combine. Garnish with an orange peel.

Spain and Portugal

Cava and Co.

"Google Maps can't find Cava, Spain." (Make sure your search is spelled correctly.)

This error message sums up the existential crisis facing Spain's most famous fizzy wine. Unlike Champagne, Cava refers not to a place but to a style of wine: namely, Spanish sparkling produced by the traditional Champagne method.

No fewer than eight autonomous communities have the legal right to label their sparkling wines with the Cava designation, including areas as remote as Aragon, Extremadura, Castile and León, Valencia, Basque Country, and La Rioja. This indifference to geographical distinctions underscores what Cava has come to represent to many modern drinkers: a cheap, fizzy import designed to lubricate wedding parties and bottomless brunches, eclipsed in popularity only by Prosecco, its chief rival.

So you'll be forgiven, then, if you have never heard of Penedès, the Catalonian region that is Cava's ancestral home. It was here, in the rolling hillsides west of Barcelona, that a man by the name of Josep Raventós effectively invented Cava in 1872, after bringing back knowledge of the Champagne method from his travels through France. And it's here that more than 95 percent of Cava continues to be made.

The Fight against "Big Cava"

How Cava went from local experiment to international brand follows a familiar twentieth-century arc. With Catalonia's rapid industrialization, what was once a modest farming culture quickly transformed into a multimillion-dollar industry aligned with the interests of a handful of bulk producers. Coupled with widespread factory farming, lax production standards, and the embrace of international grapes such as chardonnay and pinot noir, this high-volume mentality resulted in the loss of generations of local knowledge.

But if Penedès now shows signs of change, it's not because Big Cava has relaxed its stranglehold upon the region. Today, the ubiquitous Freixenet brand alone (of the black-and-gold-labeled "Cordon Negro" fame) accounts for nearly 80 percent of total Cava exports. But much like the grower rebellion that upended Champagne's established balance of power, Penedès now finds itself the battleground of a sparkling wine revolution of its own. The parallels between this emerging Catalonian counterculture and the grower uprising in Champagne are hard to ignore, involving a similar indie-versus-major-record-label struggle between growers and the big houses that still dominate production. But the situation unfolding across Cava country is more than the usual story of traditionalists upending corporate interest and returning to the soil.

Coinciding with this revival, Catalonia has emerged as an epicenter of Spain's natural wine movement, fostering a radical counterculture. The dialogue between these two factions has energized the region as a whole, inviting a deeper debate about what kind of wine tells its story best. In short, Cava has become a microcosm for the trials, tribulations, and triumphs of postmodern sparkling wine.

In fairness, there have always been Cavas that aspired toward a more expansive standard—generally vintage-dated wines labeled as gran reserva, which are aged for at least thirty months on the lees (though many winemakers opt for far longer). To some critics, however, this emphasis on process never addressed the fundamental problem of place. All too often, especially when interpreted by the large commercial Cava houses, these high-end versions read as little more than an excuse to charge a luxury premium. As a result, in the past decade many of the area's most conscientious producers have chosen to take matters into their own hands, radically rethinking what it means to make sparkling wine in Penedès.

The New Cava Isn't Called Cava

The first shot across the ideological bow came in 2012, when one influential Cava maker, Pepe Raventós of the cult Raventós i Blanc estate, outlined his plans to abandon the Cava denomination, choosing instead to adopt a regional designation of his own invention, Conca del Riu Anoia. News of this defection sent shock waves through the region, and other splinter groups soon followed, including a band of top Cava producers who formed the Corpinnat association in 2015.

Hence, the irony behind the Cava renaissance. Many of the top versions no longer bill themselves as Cava. Rather than raze the legendary category to the ground, they're trying to reframe it as a reflection of Penedès and its centuries-old culture of sparkling wine.

Along with the embrace of organic and biodynamic farming and a strict focus on the region's native grapes (from the classic Cava varieties of xarel-lo, macabeo, and parellada to such lesser-known examples as the red sumoll and trepat), much of the region's evolution mirrors Champagne's grower approach: natural grape juice in place of cane sugar to kick-start secondary fermentations; a proliferation of brut nature or zéro dosage bottlings; and the rise of single-vineyard, vintage-dated wines. The goal, of course, is not to emulate Champagne but rather to identify a style that's true to Penedès.

Consider the Corpinnat sparklers from Mas Candí, a project that began as a collaboration among vine-grower Ramón Jané; his wife, Mercè Cusco; and enologist Toni Carbó. Having sold his family's grapes to the big Cava houses for generations, Jané started bottling his own wines in 2006. A reference point for Penedès's new wave, the winery's bracingly mineral yet concentrated "Segunyola," sourced from a single parcel of sixty-year-old xarel-lo vines, exudes a palpable energy—all ripe yellow fruits and Mediterranean herbs.

Mas Candí's example is just one of many. But like many of their peers, this grower Cava framework isn't the only one in which Jané and Carbó have chosen to operate. Both belong to a growing cohort of naturalists who, through their fluency with traditional-method winemaking, are elevating pét-nat to unprecedented heights.

Penedès Pét-Nat: The Next Generation of Iberian Bubbly

Perhaps it's inevitable that Catalonia, with its deeply ingrained culture of sparkling wine, would emerge as the source of some of the most ambitious pét-nats made anywhere. No one has done more to reconceive the style than Manel Aviñó of the biodynamic Clos Lentiscus winery. Locally known as "Mr. Bubbles," Aviñó served for seventeen years as the technical director of one of the region's large Cava houses before returning to his family property to craft some of Spain's edgiest wines. While his single-parcel Champagne-method sparklers have won plenty of accolades, his elevated takes on the ancestral method have inspired a generation of practitioners, including natural-wine luminaries such as Massimo Marchiori and Antonella Gerosa of Partida Creus and Finca Parera's Rubèn Parera.

The Catalonian examples of what was once labeled a party wine require a different name, as they represent the invention of a new style of sparkling wine. In addition to disgorging for greater transparency, one of the hallmarks of Catalonia's ambitious new take on pét-nat involves unusually long aging on the lees, sometimes exceeding seven years—a practice typically associated with the great Champagne-method wines of the world but virtually unheard of for the ancestral method.

The result? Truly unclassifiable sparkling wines that combine the savory depth and complexity of top grower Cava (or, for that matter, Champagne) with the raw energy of pét-nat. It's a synthesis that could have arisen only in Penedès, where the joint insurgency against industrial winemaking has converged into something fearlessly independent and entirely its own.

PRODUCERS TO KNOW

Anima Mundi	Finca Parera
AT Roca	German Gilabert
Azimut	Loxarel
Bohigas	Mas Candí
Castellroig	Mata i Coloma
Celler la Salada	Partida Creus
Cellers de Can Suriol del Castell	Ravéntos i Blanc
Clos Lentiscus	Recaredo

The Wine List

Mata i Coloma "Cupada No. 22" Cava Brut Nature Reserva ($)

After a career consulting for conventional wineries, winemaker Pere Mata now grows five hectares of organically farmed vines in the classic Cava village of Sant Sadurní d'Anoia. This bottling offers everything you could desire from a wine at this price point, combining rich flavors of burnt lemon and candied ginger with lively acidity that keeps things fresh.

Recaredo "Terrers" Brut Nature Corpinnat ($$)

The original archetype for Alt Penedès, the arch-traditional Recaredo estate has been organically farmed since its inception in 1924. Taut and linear with a core of yellow plums, pastry dough, and scrubby herbs, its flagship Terrers is culled from several different parcels and epitomizes the domaine's vision for single-vintage brut nature wines marked by extended aging on the lees.

Clos Lentiscus "Greco di Subur" Blanc de Blancs Brut Nature ($$)

Though his groundbreaking pét-nats shouldn't be missed, Manel Aviñó's Champagne method–take on the rare malvasia de Sitges grape show-cases his mastery of classical forms. Wildly aromatic (think rosemary and thyme) and full of raw intensity, it's always one of the region's standouts, cut through with chiseled acidity and a fennel-like pop of freshness.

Anima Mundi "Noguer Baix" M. Ancestral ($$)

When he's not busy making terroir-driven Champagne-method wines, AT Roca's Agustí Torelló Roca churns out equally compelling pét-nats under his Anima Mundi label. Sourced from a single parcel of old-vine macabeo planted in 1974, his "Noguer Baix" possesses a chalky minerality and stone-fruit purity that drinks like Penedès as imagined by Champagne growers Emmanuel Lassaigne or Aurélien Lahert, no matter the difference in method.

Partida Creus "AA Anonimo" Ancestral ($$)

Winemaker Massimo Marchiori produces this pale crimson wine using different grapes from one vintage to the next. The 2018 version blends four white grapes (xarel-lo, macabeo, parellada, and moscatel) and one red (ull de llebre, aka tempranillo). Like all of its earlier releases, it's insanely drinkable, with a hibiscus-like tang and licorice-y bitterness.

Finca Parera "Mala Herba" Ancestral ($$)

For his most serious ancestral-method wine, harvested from a single parcel of old-vine xarel-lo planted high in the Alt Penedès subregion, Rubèn Parera ferments the grapes on their skins, bottles the still-fermenting juice, and then lets the wine age on the lees for two to three years before disgorgement. Though difficult to classify, the result is an apricot-scented, softly effervescent orange wine with a tea-like grip of tannins that could be a poster child for postmodern Penedès.

Txakoli

Far easier to drink than to pronounce, txakoli (also called txakolina) is the official wine of the pintxos taverns of San Sebastián, the northerly Basque equivalent of the tapas bars that proliferate farther south in the sherry country of Jerez.

While the concept behind both traditions is essentially the same (eat, sip, swallow; repeat for as long as you can remain upright), txakoli couldn't be further removed from the high-alcohol fortified realm of sherry. Intensely lean, low in alcohol, and slightly frothy, it's not a sparkling wine to be slowly contemplated and rolled over your tongue, but a young one to be recklessly chugged—ideally in traditional Basque fashion, after being poured from high above one's head into the mouth of a tumbler several feet below.

This practice, known in Spanish as escanciar (to pour out), is intended to emphasize the wine's natural effervescence. Historically, carbonation occurred naturally in the bottle after fermentation in barrel (a bit like Vinho Verde, its Portuguese equivalent). Modern txakoli, in contrast, undergoes primary fermentation in enclosed stainless-steel tanks, often under a blanket of nitrogen gas that traps CO_2 and lends the wine its signature prickle of fizz.

Made from the high-acid hondarrabi zuri and hondarrabi beltza grapes, the category arrived out of nowhere just a few years ago to secure its place in the annual rotation of go-to summer pours. The wine has become so popular that an annual txakoli fest is now held in its honor. So how did this unpronounceable beverage from a stretch of Spain better known as a tourist hot spot go on to become such a runaway hit here in the United States? That question can be answered in just three syllables: Ameztoi. One of the area's top producers, this modest family-run property almost single-handedly established txakoli's Stateside reputation.

A viral sensation from the moment it hit the market, it was the now-legendary "Rubentis" rosé that first captured the trade's attention, riding into visibility on the larger "pink wave" that forced many adventurous somms to look beyond the familiar horizons of southern France to satisfy their rosé desires. Still the category's benchmark, all sea spray and raspberry Smarties, it now sells out almost instantly each year. Happily, other equally brisk and addictive wines have followed in its wake.

The Wine List

Ameztoi Getariako Txakolina "Rubentis" Rosado ($)

Equal parts hondarrabi zuri and hondarrabi beltza, this is the breakout
txakoli that started it all. The slight spritz of CO_2, the powdered-rock
minerality, the hint of grapefruit-skin bitterness—all of these aspects
combine to form one of the most infectiously drinkable wines ever
bottled under a screw cap.

Txomin Etxaniz Getariako Txakolina ($)

Every bit a classic in its own right, Txomin Etxaniz's white Txakolina is
a textbook representation of the regional style. Made from vineyards
located just a few hundred feet from the ocean, this is a "beach read"
of a wine in the best and most literal sense.

Artomaña "Xarmant" Txakolina ($)

The fact that this zingy, zippy patio pounder from the family-run
Artomaña project is also available by the keg tells you everything you
need to know about what to expect under its screw cap. With a signature prickle of carbonation—not so much fully sparkling as almost
inadvertently fizzy—it's the kind of wine that begs to be consumed in
copious quantities.

Vinho Verde

Portugal's Vinho Verde region has forever been synonymous with lightly fizzy wines designed to be knocked back by the case. Imagine wine's answer to Key lime LaCroix and you'll have some sense of its goes-down-easy appeal.

The comparison to soda or seltzer isn't unintentional. Unlike Champagne or even Prosecco, Vinho Verde achieves its sparkle not by the traditional or Charmat methods but by simple carbonation. Industrially scaled and globally exported, this inexpensive commercial style has defined perceptions of Vinho Verde for decades. A spritzy summertime staple? For sure. One of wine's most reliable ten-buck bargains? Absolutely. But a wine that rewards sustained contemplation? Think again.

Long wed to this high-volume model, Vinho Verde is the last place you would expect to be leading the charge of Portugal's twenty-first-century renaissance. But in stark contrast to the large houses that still dominate production, a groundswell of independent winemakers has begun carving out an alternative ethos for the region. Improbably, they're making the case for what still sounds like a contradiction in terms: the rebirth of Vinho Verde as a serious wine.

Though the idea might invite snickers from wine snobs, from the standpoint of raw materials, Vinho Verde couldn't be better equipped to embody a new era of Portuguese whites. Located in the lush green hills of the nation's rainy northwest (which give the wines their name), under the cooling influence of the Minho and Lima Rivers, the area is climatically custom-built for high-acid whites. And while most of the more ambitious wines to emerge from the area of late opt to ditch the carbonation in favor of making site-expressive still wines, Vinho Verde has a long history when it comes to fizz.

That signature carbonation? It's actually a modern approximation of the cloudy, ever-so-slightly effervescent wines of Vinho Verde's past, which British author Raymond Postgate describes in his 1969 book *Portuguese Wine* as a "natural semi-sparkling wine," whose "slight prickle" arrived as a by-product of the fermentation occasionally finishing in bottle. "They taste young," he wrote. "They have the greenness of Spring."

That assessment still applies to the current generation of sparkling wines coming out of Vinho Verde today. No one has done more to plot a different future for the region than Vasco Croft, the proprietor of the biodynamically farmed Aphros estate near Ponte de Lima.

True to Vinho Verde's history, bubbles have informed the winery's approach from the start. Highlighting the area's main native grapes—loureiro, a honeysuckle-scented white, and vinhão (aka souzão), known for burly, high-acid reds—Aphros initially turned heads with piercingly pure, mineral-driven Champagne-method versions of each. More recently, though, the winery has started exploring the ancestral method with two standout pét-nats, the "Phaunus" white and rosé.

But Croft isn't the only one dreaming up a more expansive idea of Vinho Verde. Also in Ponte de Lima, António Lopes Ribeiro produces his slightly spritzy "Biotite," one of the area's highlights from organically farmed loureiro (with a smattering of the local avesso, arinto, and azal). Up north in the Melgaço subzone, on the other hand, where the alvarinho grape is king (known as albariño across the border in Spain), Quinta do Regueiro crafts a Champagne-method version. They're all proof of what's possible in Vinho Verde when someone dares to think outside the usual "cheap and cheerful" box.

PRODUCERS TO KNOW

António Lopes Ribeiro (Casa de Mouraz)	Quinta do Regueiro
Aphros	Sem Igual
Nat Cool (Niepoort)	

The Wine List

António Lopes Ribeiro Vinho Verde "Biotite" ($)

António Lopes Ribeiro always allows this loureiro-dominant, organically certified bottling to ferment spontaneously, stopping whenever nature dictates. As a result, sugar levels tend to vary from one vintage to the next; some years it finishes bone-dry, other years not so much. But it always boasts a riesling-like purity and lemon-lime lift.

Aphros 2019 Phaunus Loureiro Vinho Espumante ($)

Is it possible to depart any further from the conventional Vinho Verde stereotypes than Aphros's ancestral method "Phaunus"? Hand harvested, crushed by foot, and produced entirely without electricity, this wine spends a short time fermenting on the skins, gaining texture while still remaining faithful to the loureiro grape's delicate, floral profile.

Quinta do Regueiro Alvarinho Espumante Método Classico Bruto ($)

The Monção and Melgaço subzone has always specialized in an elevated (and typically nonsparkling) side of Vinho Verde, based entirely off the star alvarinho grape. Unusual for the area in that it employs the Champagne method of secondary fermentation in bottle, this highlights the grape's tropical side, revealing layers of kiwi and lime peel with a blast of crushed rock.

Spain and Portugal off the Beaten Path

Once upon a time, the story of sparkling wine from the Iberian Peninsula began and ended with Cava (with maybe—just *maybe*—a brief nod to Vinho Verde). Those were the same Dark Ages, of course, during which Italy was still synonymous with industrial Prosecco and France with brand-name Champagne. But the same transformation that swept through Italy and France has radically redefined the trajectory of Spanish and Portuguese bubbly, pumping fresh energy into overlooked classics while carving out plenty of new frontiers, from the moonscape-like vineyards of the Canary Islands to a raft of boundary-pushing pét-nats.

Bairrada: Portugal's Maritime Bubbly

Located in northwestern Portugal between the chilly Atlantic coast (one of the world's top surf spots) and the hillsides of the Dão region, the Bairrada area has enjoyed a modest vogue of late for tannic, long-lived reds based on the baga grape. It was here, however, that Portugal produced its first Champagne-method sparkling wine in 1890, and the area's wine industry has revolved around bubbles ever since.

Historically, local cooperatives accounted for most of Bairrada's fizzy output. Blended from baga plus high-acid whites such as Maria Gomes, arinto, and bical, this vinho espumante primarily served the purpose of washing down the region's famous suckling pig. Updating that tradition for the twenty-first century, the latest crop of talent—including rising stars such as winemaker Filipa Pato—has focused on small-scale, handcrafted versions. Typically lean, floral, and citrusy, with just enough lees-y depth to keep things complex, they offer a welcome reprieve from standard-issue industrial Cava.

PRODUCERS TO KNOW

Casa de Saima	Sidónio de Sousa
Filipa Pato	Vadio
Luis Pato	

The Canary Islands

Few vinous discoveries rival the Canary Islands for sheer strangeness. In pictures of the region, grapevines crawl out of pits of black volcanic sand, known as hoyos, that stipple the ashen landscape like craters on the moon. Adding to that sense of the surreal, during harvest it's not uncommon to spot vineyard workers hauling grapes on camelback. But what else would you expect from a subtropical island archipelago positioned seventy miles off the Moroccan coast?

Unknown to the modern wine world for decades (despite being praised by Shakespeare), the Canaries ascended to the height of fashion in the mid-2010s, when the region's tangy, smoky whites and reds captured the imagination of the progressive sommelier set. On top of an acclaimed lineup of still wines, one pioneering producer—Ignacio Valdera of the Los Bermejos project—also started experimenting with espumoso or "bubbly" versions. Bottled without dosage, both the white (based on the aromatic malvasia grape) and the rosé (from the local listán negro) have become modern classics. More recently, Pablo Matallana, the young winemaker behind the Vinicola Taro on the island of Tenerife, has come out with a head-turning malvasia-based pét-nat. It's only a matter of time before others follow.

PRODUCERS TO KNOW

| Los Bermejos | Pablo Matallana |

The New Iberian Pét-Nats

The classic Cava region of Penedès (see page 93) has emerged as Spain's most innovative pét-nat production zone, but that doesn't mean other areas aren't tinkering with the style as well. A case study in diversity, new examples continue to pop up across the country from countless indigenous grapes. This makes it difficult to point to any unifying theme, stylistic or otherwise, but that's the fun part. From Segovia, where Ismael Gozalo of MicroBio wines makes several different expressions, to Ribera del Duero (look for Alfredo Maestro's "Perdigon," sourced from a high-elevation parcel of pinot noir and garnacha) and Valencia (Bodegas Cueva is a highlight), every region puts its own stamp on the style.

One particularly promising offshoot of this trend is a nascent uprising of ancestral-method winemaking in the "sherry triangle" of Jerez. Here, Fernando Angulo of the Alba Viticultores project has dedicated himself to translating the region's famously chalky albariza soil (not unlike that of Champagne) into old-vine interpretations of the palomino fino grape. His fizzy "Campeonísimo Ancestral" is one of the area's singular expressions. Likewise, at Bodega Vinificate in Cádiz, Miguel Gómez—one of the founding partners of Alba Viticultores—has joined his brother José to produce tiny quantities of still and ancestral-method sparkling wines from several different pagos, or traditional clusters of vineyards, across the sherry triangle, such as the famous "Miraflores" in Sanlúcar de Barrameda.

A similar rehashing of tradition is also underway in Portugal's classic Douro region, the historic home of fortified port. Along with his celebrated still wines, all sourced from vineyards traditionally used for port production, winemaker Tiago Sampaio has also introduced a lineup of pét-nats under his Folias de Baco label.

PRODUCERS TO KNOW

Alba Viticultores	Bodegas Cerro la Barca
Alfredo Maestro	Bodegas Cueva
Bodega Vinificate	Vinificate Amorro

The Wine List

Filipa Pato Bairrada Brut Rosé "3B" ($)

Filipa Pato brings a low-intervention philosophy (vinhos autênticos sem maquilhagem, or "authentic wines without makeup," as she puts it on the label) to this refreshing bubbly rosé. The three *B*'s of the title stand for the native grapes baga and bical, plus her home region of Bairrada, but she might consider adding another *B* for bargain, as this bottling consistently over-delivers for its modest price tag.

Los Bermejos Espumoso Malvasía Brut Nature ($)

If there's one thing that Canary Islands whites never lack it's mineral complexity, but eighteen months spent aging on the lees only amplifies the salinity and smoky volcanic quality of this traditional-method interpretation of malvasia. Using grape juice (rather than sugar) to kick-start the secondary fermentation, it balances that "in your face" power with plenty of floral perfume.

Bodega Vinificate Mahara Aguja Colipinta Ancestral ($)

Stemming from the famed Miraflores vineyard in the legendary sherry-producing town of Sanlúcar de Barrameda, Bodega Vinificate's ancestral method "Aguja Colipinta" shines a fresh light on the area's classic palomino grape and chalky albariza soils. Displaying the same maritime saltiness found in the best dry sherries, it also reveals a slightly nutty character—a stylistic nod to Andalusia's oxidative winemaking traditions.

Folias de Baco PT NAT Branco ($)

One of the main architects of the alt Douro movement, Tiago Sampaio prizes finesse over force. Of his three pét-nats, the Branco—a mind-bending mix of indigenous white varieties, including arinto, rabigato, and moscatel galego—might just be the best, combining the region's schist minerality with tangy grapefruit and pear.

Sidónio de Sousa Branco Brut Nature ($)

Yet another attention-worthy effort from a country whose capacity for value seems to know no bounds, this blend of Bairrada's native bical, Maria Gomes, and arinto grapes packs more wine into a fifteen-dollar package than anyone could reasonably expect. Proof that there's life beyond industrial Cava, it's clean and lemony with a refreshing whiff of crushed mint.

Alfredo Maestro Pét-Nat "Perdigón" ($)

Best known for his high-altitude reds from blockbuster grapes such as garnacha and tinto fino (aka tempranillo), Alfredo Maestro makes this bone-dry rosado pét-nat primarily from a young parcel of pinot noir planted in the hills north of Valencia. Always surprisingly delicate and reminiscent of wild strawberries, it represents Spanish minimalism at its finest.

A History of Sparkling Wine

1531

Monks in Abbey of Saint-Hilaire, in the Limoux region, invent the world's first sparkling wine, now Blanquette de Limoux, made in the ancestral method.

1729

Ruinart, the oldest established Champagne house, is founded.

1892

Paul Masson released his first "California Champagne."

1895

Federico Martinotti, a Piedmontese, patents the tank, or Marinotti, method (further developed by Frenchman Eugène Charmat in 1910), paving the way for the modern Prosecco boom.

1969

Riunite corporation establishes an outpost in the United States, sparking the Lambrusco craze of the 1970s.

1979

Krug creates the first single-vineyard Champagne, its iconic Clos du Mesnil.

1816

Madame Clicquot of Veuve Clicquot invents the riddling process to remove yeast after secondary fermentation, resulting in the first méthode champenoise wine.

1872

Josep Raventós makes the first traditional-method wine in Penedès, Catalonia, under the Cordoníu label, called Champán (eventually becoming Cava).

1961

First Franciacortia sparkling wine is made by Guido Berlucchi winery.

1965

Jack and Jamie Davies purchase Schramsberg Vineyards in Calistoga, California.

Early to mid-1990s

The first "Grower Champagnes" begin to arrive in the US market, thanks to the work of boutique importers such as Terry Theise, Kermit Lynch, and several others.

Late 1990s

Christian Chaussard coins the term *pét-nat* in France's Loire Valley.

Germany and Austria

Germany

In the Teutonic tradition, the term for sparkling wine is Sekt, and for much of the previous century, it was difficult to decide which was worse: the reputation of the wines themselves or the litany of double entendres they inspire among English-language wine writers?

Though Germany and Austria both consume prodigious quantities of sparkling wine—for several years running, the Germans have led the globe in per capita consumption—neither nation boasts the greatest modern track record for making it. *Modern* is the operative word, however. If we look back to the nineteenth-century golden age of German and Austrian wine, a completely different picture emerges.

By the end of the 1800s, German Sekt—or Deutscher Champagner, as it was dubbed at the time—regularly graced the tables of royalty and often fetched higher prices than Champagne. In fact, several leading Champagne houses, including such storied names as Krug, Bollinger, and Piper-Heidsieck, were originally born of German parentage. For its part, Austria's fizzy heritage extends back just as far, when it was the toast of monocle-clad archdukes and counts throughout the Austro-Hungarian Empire.

This fall from grace follows a familiar twentieth-century arc: back-to-back world wars, economic recession, and the nosedive of quality that always occurs after a shift to industrial production. Abandoning the far more costly traditional method of secondary fermentation in bottle, both nations quickly switched to the Charmat method of refermentation in giant pressurized tanks to flood the market with millions of gallons of cheap, semisweet bubbly.

For these reasons, little German or Austrian sparkling wine reached US shores until recently. Deeply entrenched public skepticism toward wine from the two countries certainly didn't improve the situation. (For the record, they're not categorically sweet!) But after a recent wave of lobbying from influential US sommeliers, Germany and Austria have finally started generating the sort of excitement befitting two of the world's oldest wine cultures. Though still niche by even the most generous standards, Sekt accounts for a small but growing part of that reevaluation.

Ever since Prussian officials began ranking Germany's top vineyards in the nineteenth century, German wine enthusiasts have worshipped the country's top riesling vineyards with the same cultish obsession lavished upon any of the legendary wines of France. If you're already one of the converted, then the country's capacity for riveting sparkling wine makes perfect sense.

The apotheosis of cool-climate transparency and site specificity, German wine—and in particular, German riesling—is every terroir fanatic's dream come true, making it an endless subject of study and debate. At the northernmost limits of European viticulture, the steep, terraced vineyards that rise from the banks of the Mosel and Rhine Rivers (and their various tributaries) have historically waged an epic struggle for ripeness, even relying upon the heat and light reflected off of the surface of the water to ensure that grapes reach peak maturity. Low in alcohol yet dazzling in their complex depth, the wines born out of this battle exude a palpable tension among electric acidity, stony minerality, and succulent fruit that acts as a perfect tuning fork for transmitting the nuances of the soil. Unsurprisingly, these very same qualities add up to a uniquely German style of sparkling wine that couldn't be replicated anywhere else.

Today Sekt is made in several German regions using an array of different grapes, from pinot noir, or spätburgunder (rising star Eva Fricke's is one of the best), to local oddities such as elbling, scheurebe, and mus-kateller. But German wine's claim to fame has always rested upon the incomparable greatness of its riesling, and its Sekt expressions prove no exception. With its aromatic lift, concentrated fruit, and off-the-charts acidity, German Sekt delivers the same master class in terroir distinctions as its still counterparts, offering yet another lens for examining the particularities of place.

A great intro to the category would be the vertigo-inducing slopes of the Mosel, home to what many consider Germany's greatest riesling. In recent years, a handful of the region's progressive producers—from Erich Weber of Hofgut Falkenstein and Weingut Peter Lauer's Florian Lauer to Immich-Batterieberg's Gernot Kollmann—have been working to define a distinctly Mosel Sekt style. Consider Lauer's laser-focused riesling Sekt, sourced primarily from the gray slate hillside of the celebrated Ayler Kupp vineyard in the Saar, a subregion of the Mosel. With its piercing freshness and cleansing wash of bubbles, it delivers the same burst of lime zest and white flowers with a savory, wet-stone element found across his acclaimed still versions from the site.

For a counterpoint to the austerity and rigor of the Mosel and Saar, the riesling-based Sekts from the warmer Pfalz and Nahe regions, and even certain examples from the Rheingau, tend to showcase a slightly riper, ampler side of the grape. Of course, we're talking about relative degrees of amplitude here; it is, after all, still riesling.

PRODUCERS TO KNOW

Eva Fricke	Von Buhl
Hofgut Falkenstein	Von Winning
Immich-Batterieberg	Weingut Leitz
Maximin Grünhäuser	Weingut Matthias Hild
Robert Weil	Weingut Peter Lauer
Schlossgut Diel	Weiser-Künstler
Stein	

Austria

The Austrian Sekt story officially begins in 1842, when Robert Alwin Schlumberger, then the cellar master of the historic Ruinart Champagne house, married the daughter of a wealthy Viennese factory owner and followed her to Austria to establish the country's first major sparkling wine firm. Still cranking out millions of bottles per year, the Sektkellerei Schlumberger effectively coined the "big business" model that would define Austria's Sekt industry for the next 150 years.

It wasn't until 1976, when Austria's supreme court granted Gerald Malat of the Kremstal region's Malat winery the right to make sparkling wine from his own grapes, that the country saw its first estate-bottled Winzersekt (or "grower Sekt," if you will). Others soon followed, including the influential Bründlmayer winery in the neighboring Kamptal region; within just a few decades, the areas emerged as the epicenter of Austria's modern Sekt revolution.

It's only fitting that the Kamptal and Kremstal regions have become an incubator for the country's most ambitious sparklers. Along with the Wachau—not a traditional hot spot for sparkling wine and thus omitted here—they are the top sources for the country's showstopping rieslings and grüner veltliners. As in Germany, many of the same benchmark estates behind the area's legendary still wines have also raised the bar for its world-class bubbly.

In addition to pioneers such as Bründlmayer, Steininger, Loimer, and Schloss Gobelsburg (all key players in the development of grower Sekt), the Kamptal is now home to younger talents such as Alwin Jurtschitsch (the natural-wine Wunderkind behind one of Austria's penetrating rosés) and Martin and Anna Arndorfer, also repping the region's minimalist revolution. Kremstal highlights include the Malat estate, as well as Weingut Nigl (check out its textured, lemon curd–scented "Blanc de Blancs Brut," assembled from equal parts grüner veltliner and chardonnay), and up-and-comer Christoph Hoch, who crafts a standout Champagne-method sparkler from pinot blanc (as well as a bunch of pét-nats, but more on that later).

If it's somewhat challenging to identify a stylistic common denominator that unites all of these producers' wines, that's in part a reflection of the varied grape varieties at their disposal. Beyond the usual riesling and grüner veltliner, that umbrella extends to international varieties such as chardonnay and various pinots (noir, blanc, and gris), plus native reds, like the bright, light-bodied zweigelt and St. Laurent. Depending on the blend, this mix of raw materials affords winemakers plenty of creative leeway. The result? Everything from lively, aromatic wines showcasing riesling and grüner veltliner to richer, creamier versions incorporating (to varying degrees) the classic grapes of Champagne, plus full-bodied blanc de noirs and plenty of zippy yet structured rosé.

Finally, it's worth mentioning Austria's other, oft-overlooked Sekt zone. Though relatively unknown today, the Weinviertel area—a large swathe of vineyards northeast of the iconic zones of Wachau, Kamptal, and Kremstal—historically operated as grape supplier of base wines for Austria's large sparkling wine houses. In the northernmost (and chilliest) corner of the region, however, right across from the Czech border, Champagne-trained winemaker Christian Madl is making some of the country's most intriguing sparkling wines, including a zéro dosage, 100 percent grüner veltliner that spends more than thirty-six months aging on the lees.

PRODUCERS TO KNOW

Bründlmayer	Malat
Christian Madl	Martin & Anna Arndorfer
Christoph Hoch	Schloss Gobelsburg
Fred Loimer	Weingut Nigl
Jurtschitsch	

The Wine List

Weingut Peter Lauer Riesling Sekt ($$)

A master of the Saar subzone's ethereal cast of rieslings, winemaker Florian Lauer brings the same transparency and site sensitivity to this vintage-dated Sekt that informs all of his critically acclaimed wines. Though it boasts penetrating linearity, it's anything but austere, with loads of pear and a lacy, almost imperceptible sweetness.

Immich-Batterieberg "Jour Fixe" Riesling Brut Zéro ($$$)

Here's a German Sekt for fans of racy, high-acid, zéro dosage Champagne. The Immich-Batterieberg take on the genre comes from three different parcels of extremely old-vine riesling (Ellergrub, Zollturm, and Oberemmeler Altenberg), giving it a breadth and concentration that belie its low 12 percent alcohol level.

Von Winning Riesling Sekt ($)

The Von Winning estate's Riesling Sekt Extra Brut, grown on clay and red sandstone in the Pfalz village of Deidesheim, exudes a clean, lemony tang with warm flavors of nectarine and spice (courtesy of said sandstone). Infinitely versatile, it's the kind of outside-the-box bubbly you don't have to think twice about popping on a random Tuesday night.

Eva Fricke Sekt Pinot Noir Rosé Brut Nature ($$)

Thanks to climate change, Germany's famously marginal wine regions have developed a knack for growing pinot noir. In the hands of star winemaker Eva Fricke, who has been breathing fresh energy into the canonical Rheingau area, the grape is channeled into a delicate and mineral-etched Sekt rosé that compares favorably with any version from France.

Schloss Gobelsburg Sekt Brut Reserve ($$)

The flagship nonvintage bubbly from one of Austria's Sekt pioneers, this creamy yet aromatic effort combines what Austrians call blauburgunder (pinot noir to you and me) with a touch of native riesling and grüner veltliner for good measure. Two to three years of aging on the lees imparts a creaminess that doesn't distract from the piercing purity of its fruit.

Jurtschitsch Brut Sekt Rosé ($$)

Alwin Jurtschitsch of the family-run Jurtschitsch estate in Langenlois takes a decidedly hands-off approach (no chemical sprays, natural yeast fermentations, zero additives) to craft terroir-driven wines that rank among Austria's best. The only sparkling wine in his portfolio, his Zweigelt-based traditional-method rosé cranks up the freshness to ten (imagine one of those Ocean Spray commercials from the 1980s).

Christoph Hoch "Kalkreich" Sekt ($)

The only traditional-method sparkling wine from the Kremstal's self-appointed master of pét-nat, Christoph Hoch's nonvintage "Kalkreich" comes from the family's thirty-five-year-old plantings of pinot blanc, with a touch of riesling and grüner veltliner. Refermented using grape must of the same vintage and aged in the bottle for thirty-six months, it walks a perfect tightrope between lees-y richness and the low-alcohol freshness that is Hoch's hallmark.

Natural Bubbly in Germany and Austria

Given their stereotypically Teutonic reputations for technical excellence and precision engineering, Germany and Austria are probably the last places you'd presume to find thriving natural-wine scenes. Paradoxically, though, both have attracted a great deal of naturalist activity of late, most of it centered in less-established areas that offer greater license to experiment. That momentum has given rise to a fascinating wave of wines from unexpected places, including a growing influx of Austro-Germanic pét-nat.

The German Outliers

Once we venture beyond Germany's classic riesling strongholds (notably, the Mosel and Rheingau), an undiscovered universe of possibilities opens up. Darlings of the natural-wine bars of Berlin, the cabal of winemakers leading the movement—including names such as 2Naturkinder and Weingut Brand, among others—has brought fresh attention to grapes and growing areas that never entered the official narrative about German wine. From Franken (or Franconia, home of the racy silvaner grape) to the southern territories of Baden (an increasingly fashionable source of light-bodied pinot noir) and Württemberg, where the little-known trollinger grape (among others) has gained an improbable industry foothold, the country is now awash in alternative bubbles that illustrate German minimalism at its best.

PRODUCERS TO KNOW

2Naturkinder	Weingut Gold
Weingut Brand	

The Austrian Avant-Garde

Meanwhile, Austria has spawned a counterculture of its own. Far from the regal estates of Wachau, Kamptal, and Kremstal, the Burgenland area, bordering Hungary, has racked up a lot of hipster currency as a breeding ground for naturalist riffs on the area's red-skinned blaufränk-isch, Zweigelt, and St. Laurent grapes, plus a smattering of local whites. The ancestral-method versions come in all colors and number among Austria's best.

Then there's Steiermark (or Styria), Austria's second-smallest and least-populated winemaking region, nestled above the densely forested Slovenian border. Another bastion of low-impact winemaking, it's here that natural-wine legend Franz Strohmeier produces some of Austria's best sparkling wines, though not strictly in the ancestral method. Along with his cloudy "Sekt Weiss," an undisgorged blend of chardonnay and sauvignon blanc that undergoes secondary fermentation in bottle, he's best known for his head-turning "Schilcher," an outré take on the area's traditional rosé.

PRODUCERS TO KNOW

Claus Preisinger	Pittnauer
Fuchs und Hase	Strohmeier
Hager Matthias	Weingut Judith Beck
Meinklang	

The Wine List

Weingut Brand Pét-Nat Blanc ($)

Based in the village of Bockenheim in the northernmost reaches of the Pfalz, brothers Daniel and Jonas Brand have skyrocketed to renown as poster children of the new German avant-garde. Equal parts silvaner and weissburgunder (aka pinot blanc) from thirty-year-old, organically farmed vines, this one clocks in at a mere 10 percent alcohol, typifying the hyper-lean, stripped-down aesthetic that has become German pét-nat's calling card.

2Naturkinder Silvaner Pét-Nat ($)

The "two natural children" in question are husband-and-wife team Michael Völker and Melanie Drese, who migrated from London to the countryside of Franken in 2013. This is classic silvaner country, and here the overlooked German grape makes for an uncommonly elegant pét-nat, all white flowers and celery stalk with a whisper of white peppercorn.

Weingut Gold "Pink Gold" ($)

Riding a wider wave of interest in crushable, goes-down-easy reds, the juicy trollinger grape emerged as the focal point of a wider surge of interest in the wines of Germany's southwestern region of Baden. This effort from avid naturalist Leon Gold channels everything there is to love about the grape into a delightful pét-nat package bursting with raspberry seed, rose petals, and rhubarb.

Claus Preisinger St. Laurent "Ancestral" ($)

There's clearly a touch of the mad scientist about Claude Preisinger. From his (roughly) forty-six acres of vines in Austria's Burgenland, he produces a dizzying number of wines each year in just about every conceivable style, including this curious ancestral-method take on the St. Laurent grape. Technically a sparkling rosé, this leans more toward a blanc de noirs in style, with its pale onion-skin color and tart grapefruit flavors.

Strohmeier Schilcher Frizzante ($$)

A local specialty of Austria's Styria region, the fizzy rosé known as Schilcher is based on the high-acid blauer wildbacher grape. Frank Strohmeier puts a natty twist on the category with this garnet-hued, crown-capped frizzante version that goes down with a pleasant lambic-like tang.

Weingut Judith Beck "Pét-Nat M Bambule!" ($)

The oddball Muskat Ottonel variety shares the stage with the equally idiosyncratic neuberger in this disgorged pét-nat from Judith Beck, one of several she makes under the experimental Bambule! banner. This one's salty and peachy, with all the aromatic fireworks you'd expect from the muscat family of grapes.

From Dry to Sweet

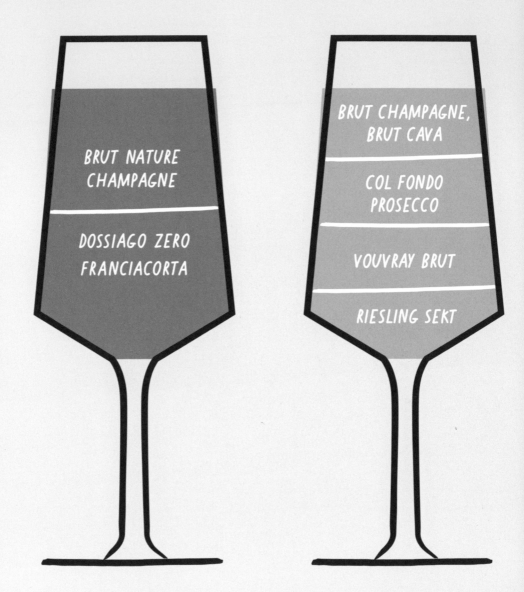

Bone Dry

BRUT NATURE
CHAMPAGNE

DOSSIAGO ZERO
FRANCIACORTA

Fully Dry

BRUT CHAMPAGNE,
BRUT CAVA

COL FONDO
PROSECCO

VOUVRAY BRUT

RIESLING SEKT

PROSECCO

DEMI-SEC
CHAMAPGNE

BUGEY-CERDON

BRACHETTO D'ACQUI

MOSCATO D'ASTI

Dryish to Off Dry

Semisweet to Fully Sweet

NORTH SEA

IRISH SEA

KENDAL

WHITBY

LEEDS

PLYMOUTH

BRIGHTON

England

What Is English about English Sparkling Wine?

Throughout history, the English have been some of the world's most prolific wine drinkers. Shakespeare's Falstaff famously delighted in a "good sherris sack," while Charles Dickens had a personal penchant for Sauternes, Chablis, and Metternich hock, as revealed by a handwritten inventory of his cellar. Then there is Sir Winston Churchill, whose love of drink is both notorious and well documented; he reportedly claimed that the four essentials of life were "hot baths, cold Champagne, new peas, and old brandy."

If the iconic statesman had been born just a few generations later, he wouldn't have needed to look to France for the bubbly stuff. To anyone who has been keeping track, the sudden rise of England as a top producer of terroir-driven sparkling wines represents one of the most unexpected success stories of recent memory. In the words of English writer Andrew Jefford, "What had once been regarded as a harmless eccentricity has become, over the last decade, one of the wine world's most promising developments."

Even just a few decades ago, to speak of an English wine industry would have represented wishful thinking. Up until the 1970s, the country's efforts amounted to little more than a cottage industry, planted to lesser German varieties and hybrid grapes that stood the best chance of ripening. In the late 1980s and early 1990s, however, a few visionary producers—notably, the pioneering Nyetimber estate, which remains one of England's top wineries—took a bet on planting chardonnay, pinot noir, and pinot meunier, the classic grapes of Champagne.

Unlike many aspirational sparkling wine regions, which typically adopt those varieties by default, in England's case the decision was based on sound logic. Remember the White Cliffs of Dover, one of the United Kingdom's most famous landmarks? Well, they owe their existence to the same ridge of chalky limestone that runs directly across the English Channel and into the prime southeast English vineyard areas of Sussex, Kent, and Hampshire. Lately, as climate change continues to boost ripeness levels in the vines, making it possible to cultivate perfectly ripe grapes, this unexpected corner of England has been transformed into prime sparkling wine real estate. It didn't take long for the rest of the world to notice, especially after the wines started snatching up top prizes and trophies in global competitions over the past few years, even sometimes outperforming top Champagnes.

Above all, the essential hallmark of the English style is an almost electric freshness. Not the usual run-of-the-mill, cool-climate freshness that we associate with any number of places, but an extreme sort of freshness—like that of Champagne, but with the acidity turned up to ten. Although individual wineries tend to interpret this profile through their particular stylistic lens, there's no denying that Britain now lays claim to its very own sparkling expression. In an increasingly uncertain post-Brexit world, at least there's that to celebrate.

PRODUCERS TO KNOW

Exton Park	Hattingly Valley
Gusbourne	Nyetimber
Harrow & Hope	Wiston Estate

The Wine List

Gusbourne Blanc de Blancs ($$)

A brilliant take on the blanc de blancs style sourced from 100 percent estate-grown fruit, this vintage-designated cuvée represents the flagship wine of the celebrated Gusbourne estate. Aged for thirty-six months on the lees, its textural depth is balanced by a powerful minerality, making it a perfect "oyster wine."

Harrow & Hope Brut Reserve ($$)

The flagship blend from one of England's top family-run estates, this blend of the classic Champagne varieties comprises 20 percent reserve wines, lending a surprising complexity. It's lemony and bright, with a quintessentially English mineral streak.

Exton Park Pinot Noir Rosé ($$)

This pale, salmon-hued rosé from Hampshire-based Exton Park—a blend of 70 percent pinot noir and 30 percent pinot meunier—exhibits a cool-climate transparency that conjures the famous South Downs chalk on which it's grown. Though delicate, it still packs a punch of flavor, with notes of crunchy cranberry.

The United States of America

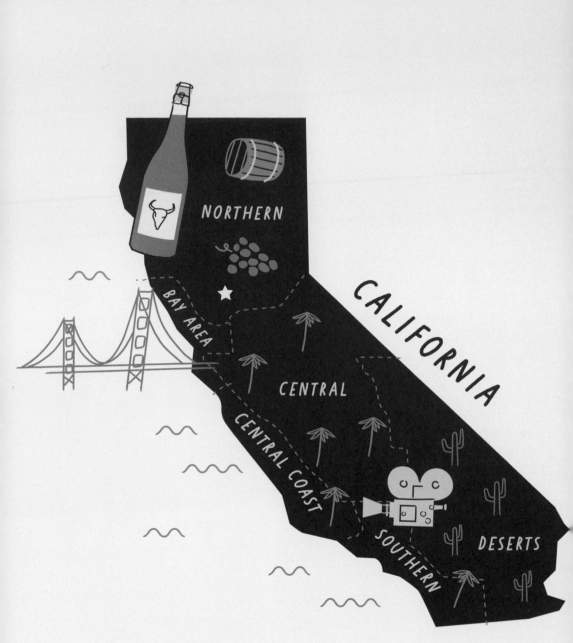

California Doesn't Do "Champagne"

Ever since 1892, when Burgundy expat Paul Masson released his first "California Champagne," the prospect of producing sparkling wine in the Golden State has entailed one thing: imitation of the French original. That was true before Prohibition, when large firms such as Masson's enjoyed a booming local business. And with the exception of cheap carbonated brands, like André and Korbel (best left as distant memories of dorm-room hangovers), Champagne would continue to set the standard for the state's sparkling wine ambitions for decades to come.

That debt should come as no surprise—not least because many of California's major sparkling wine houses (Mumm Napa, Domaine Carneros, Domaine Chandon, and Roederer Estate, among others) were founded in the 1970s and 1980s by actual Champagne companies. Along with homegrown efforts such as Calistoga's Schramsberg Vineyards, which has crafted Champagne-styled wines in the traditional method since 1965, and Sonoma's Iron Horse Vineyards (in the bubbly market since 1980), these large firms churn out millions of bottles per year according to the same grand marque (major brand) model exported from France.

By sourcing grapes from across the state and blending multiple vintages to achieve a consistent house style, the strategy behind that approach—whether executed on French turf or exported to sunny California—is to produce a reliable product over one that might reflect place. And in fairness, reliability is exactly what the market demanded. Like the big Champagne houses that inspired them, over the years these California stalwarts perfected that time-honored system. In particular, Schramsberg and Roederer remain the clear reference points for this old-school paradigm. Typically a touch rounder and fleshier than anything you'd expect from northeastern France, with riper, more caramelized fruit flavors, their wines conjure classic blended Champagne as it might taste with California's average annual hours of sunshine.

There's nothing to dislike, in other words, about a wine such as Roederer Estate's entry-level nonvintage "Brut" bottling (still a steal at under thirty dollars per bottle), or Schramsberg's vintage-dated "J. Schram" label, the winery's answer to Cristal and Dom Pérignon (other than the steep price tag, perhaps). But at a time when sparkling wine is being reconsidered globally—not as a wine style unto itself but as just another way to express the particularities of place—it has often felt like California somehow missed the memo, reflecting a mainstream that even Champagne itself has since outgrown.

That is, until now. From a recent spate of site-specific bottlings inspired by Champagne's grower revolution to a new crop of innovative and unorthodox pét-nats, the current generation of Golden State talent is raising a long overdue question: What would it take to create a uniquely Californian sparkling wine idiom that reflects the full depth and diversity of what California is today?

The New California Sparkling Wine

The first signs that California might be entering a new bubbly era surfaced in 2014, when a single bottle rode a viral wave of acclaim to instant cult status. On paper, Michael Cruse's Ultramarine project, which the former chemistry major operates out of his custom-built warehouse in Petaluma, might read like a modern update to California's decades-old crush on Champagne.

To that end, Cruse's approach as a sparkling winemaker has been shaped by his visits with revered growers such as Jérôme Prévost, Marie-Noëlle Ledru, and Alexandre Chartogne of Chartogne-Taillet, and much of the initial hype surrounding Ultramarine fed off this California-goes-grower backstory. Like his favorite Champagnes, the wines that Cruse makes under his Ultramarine label are sourced from single vineyards, fermented with ambient yeasts, vintage dated, and bottled with the addition of little, if any, dosage. But the ultimate lesson that Cruse—along with a handful of peers, including Sonoma's Under the Wire project, Berkeley's Hammerling Wines, and Wenzlau in the Santa Rita Hills—learned from his French mentors transcends mere imitation.

Sure, they might take certain cues from their French heroes, such as decreasing dosage levels (too much sugar, the thinking goes, risks obscuring place), bottling at lower pressures (according to some, less aggressive carbonation better highlights a wine's underlying character), and generally following a minimally invasive agenda (insofar as that's possible with the technically demanding Champagne method). But each of these decisions serves the same purpose: determining what, exactly, their dirt has to say.

That's all the more evident as winemakers increasingly gravitate toward cooler, marginal growing areas that, in their view, offer the promise of more balanced, terroir-driven wines. That mission is what drove Morgan Twain-Peterson—who has been making a lineup of single-vineyard, single-vintage sparklers under his Under the Wire label since 2014—to remote sites such as the Brosseau Vineyard in the Monterey appellation of Chalone, planted eighteen hundred feet above sea level, and the foggy, windswept Hirsch Vineyards in the far Sonoma Coast. It's also what accounts for the chiseled purity and salinity of Wenzlau Vineyard's "Cuvée L'Inconnu," from the family estate's Wente Block parcel located six miles from the Pacific. And it's what Joshua Hammerling has in mind when he describes the "tortured chardonnay" from the Manchester Ridge Vineyard, perched two thousand feet up in the mountains of Mendocino, that provides what he calls the "mineral-driven, oyster-shell quality" of his "Let's Get Lost" blanc de blancs.

As portraits of their respective sites, many of which have never been rendered in fizzy form, these wines offer a fresh perspective on California's potential. In many cases, that mandate doesn't even require sticking to the usual Champagne grapes. One of Under the Wire's most intriguing efforts is a sparkling zinfandel (arguably the most Californian of California grapes) from Twain-Peterson's one-hundred-year-old Bedrock Heritage vineyard in Sonoma. Equally unexpected is the traditional-method albariño, a white variety native to Spain's Galicia region that Dan and Jacqueline Person make under their bubbles-centric Carboniste label.

Pét-Nat and the California Avant-Garde

Always one step ahead of the cultural mainstream, California has also given us some of the United States' most compelling examples of pét-nat. Early touchstones, including Donkey & Goat's Lily's Cuvée or Birichino's tangy, saline Malvasia, have since become benchmarks in their own right. However, anyone who has thrown back a crown-capped bottle of the stuff knows that the wines aren't often crafted for contemplation. That's all part of the allure. But many of California's producers are challenging that notion, both in theory and practice.

Consider a wine like Scar of the Sea's "Solera Méthode Ancestrale" chardonnay from the celebrated Bien Nacido Vineyards, which includes a percentage of multivintage reserve wine and might be best understood as a postmodern hybrid between pét-nat and nonvintage Champagne. With its layers of savory nuance, the result is unlike any other pét-nat in the market today—French, domestic, or anywhere else. And yet there's something undeniably Californian in the way the technique evokes Bien Nacido's maritime influence, amplifying a pungent salinity that, despite plenty of marketing spin to the contrary, isn't always apparent in still versions of the site.

Along similar lines, few have worked harder to elevate the ancestral method than Michael Cruse, who brings the same rigor that informs Ultramarine to the range of affordable table wines he crafts under his Cruse Wine Co. label. In addition to "Tradition," a Champagne-method sparkler blended from three separate cool-climate vineyards, the Cruse lineup contains a handful of pét-nats that reflect a discipline seldom associated with the technique. Whereas classic pét-nat trades upon the "natural" part of its name, telegraphing a rusticity via cloudiness and funk, Cruse is one of a growing number of producers, including Scar of the Sea and Blue Ox, who disgorge their pét-nats, removing the deposit of yeast that has come to be seen as the style's calling card. To him, the choice offers a way "to examine a site with greater purity" while also challenging the conventional wisdom that has maintained the superiority of the Champagne method.

In 2018, for example, he made a pét-nat of valdiguié, one of those long-lost California grapes that's now making a comeback, from Napa's Rancho Chimiles vineyard. The following year, however, responding to his sense of the vintage, he opted to make a traditional-method version instead. Both wines speak to the truth of that place, just in different ways.

It's the unregulated sense of possibility and improvisation that is perhaps the defining feature of California's new perspective on sparkling wine. After decades of comparisons to somewhere so far away, it's all part of figuring out what "here" is supposed to taste like.

PRODUCERS TO KNOW

Birichino	Maître de Chai
Carboniste	Scar of the Sea
Caraccioli Cellars	Schramsberg Vineyards
Cruse Wine Co.	Ultramarine
Donkey & Goat	Under the Wire
Hammerling Wines	Wenzlau Vineyard
Los Pilares	

The Wine List

Cruse Wine Co. "Tradition" Sparkling Wine ($$)

Ultramarine might get all the hype, but Michael Cruse's work under the Cruse Wine Co. label is just as essential, providing a more affordable entry point into his vision for California. A chardonnay-dominant blend from the Rorick Vineyard in the Sierra Foothills, Rita's Crown Vineyard in Santa Barbara, and Mendocino's Alder Springs Vineyard, his aptly named "Tradition" bottling, made in the traditional method, presents a bigger-picture view of what California looks like in bubbly form. It's full of sunny fruit and lemon rind, with a mellow but vivacious wash of bubbles.

Hammerling Wines "Sunflower Sutra" California Sparkling Wine ($$)

Among the most promising members of California's sparkling renaissance, Joshua Hammerling makes a range of single-vineyard wines that act as snapshots of one particular place. The idea for his "Sunflower Sutra" bottling, however, involves sourcing the traditional Champagne grapes (pinot meunier, pinot noir, and chardonnay) from a handful of organic and dry-farmed vineyards, then channeling them into a California-wide remix of classic blended Champagne. Twelve months of pre-disgorgement bottle aging lend this a bit of backbone, but it's all about high-toned fruit, plus an herbal accent (marjoram and eucalyptus) that you'd never mistake as coming from northeastern France.

Wenzlau Vineyard "Cuvée L'Inconnu" Blanc de Blancs ($$$)

It was none other than Cindy and Bill Wenzlau's friend Cédric Bouchard, the high priest of grower Champagne, who, upon tasting chardonnay grapes from their organically farmed family vineyard, recognized the site's potential for exceptional sparkling wine. That initial suggestion has since given birth to one of California's most bracingly mineral traditional-method efforts, bearing the imprint of the chilly Pacific coast above which it is grown.

Under the Wire "Bedrock Vineyard" Old Vine Sparkling Zinfandel ($$$)

Under the Wire's interpretation of Morgan Twain-Peterson's Bedrock site (planted in 1888) exposes a more delicate side of old-vine Sonoma zin in the form of a golden-hued blanc de noirs. You can taste the age of those vines in its intense concentration of citrus and fennel flavors and its snappy spine of acids.

Scar of the Sea "Solera Méthode Ancestrale" Bien Nacido Chardonnay ($$)

According to winemaker Mikey Giugni, Scar of the Sea's genre-bending bubbly from the famous Bien Nacido Vineyards in Santa Maria Valley pays homage to Bérêche's Reflet d'Antan bottling, a nonvintage Champagne that's produced through a similar process of fractional blending. In a radical departure from standard pét-nat protocol, more than half of the base material for this wine comprises a mix of vintages dating back to 2014. With its surprising layers of umami, it cracks the category wide open.

OREGON

OREGON COAST

METRO

WILLIAMETTE
VALLEY

CENTRAL

EASTERN

SOUTHERN

Oregon

In 1965, when David Lett, the late founder of the Willamette Valley's Eyrie Vineyards, planted Oregon's first commercial pinot noir vines, the odds seemed stacked against him. According to conventional wisdom, the future of the US wine industry belonged to California; the prospect of growing grapes north of the state line invited a heavy dose of serious skepticism, if not outright mockery.

But like all visionaries, Lett had an important hunch: that the chilly Pacific Northwest could become a perfect breeding ground for world-class pinot noir (as well as some pretty impressive chardonnay and pinot gris). We now know, of course, that his hunch paid off exponentially: within the span of just five decades, Oregon—and the famous Willamette Valley, in particular—has established itself as a premier destination for the grape. If the state initially fashioned its ambitions after the legendary wines of Burgundy, it wouldn't be too long before the realization dawned that the same qualities that brought critical attention to its still wines might translate to some seriously classy bubbles as well.

That movement began in earnest with the Argyle Winery in Dundee, a producer of traditional-method sparkling wines since 1987. Known for extensively lees-aged interpretations of the classic Champagne grapes of pinot noir, chardonnay, and pinot meunier, Argyle remains the state's fizzy benchmark. Though others would follow, including modern-day icons such as Soter Vineyards in the Yamhill-Carlton area, only recently has Oregon's sparkling wine scene truly come into its own. Like their Californian counterparts, the alt Oregon producers leading this renaissance have introduced a brilliant outpouring of fizzy wines in a multitude of styles.

Consider Steven Thompson and Kris Fade's biodynamically farmed Analemma winery, based in the Columbia Gorge area. Having initially made waves with takes on albariño and mencia—grapes native to the verdant maritime clime of northwestern Spain's Galicia region—Analemma's traditional-method "Atavus" Blanc de Noirs, first released in 2014, has become a poster bottle for Oregon bubbly's new wave. Conjuring a completely different referent point, Brooks winery reinterprets Oregon through the lens of German Sekt with its bone-dry traditional-method riff on Willamette Valley riesling.

These are just two examples of many. In the meantime, Oregon's alternative crowd has been busy crafting some of the country's edgiest experiments with the ancestral method, using a motley crew of grapes that speak to an explosion of disparate influences. In particular, given the French region's comparably damp climate and its claim to fame as the beating heart of France's natural wine movement, many local practitioners of the style have drawn inspiration from the iconic pét-nats of the Loire Valley, but the trend now transcends any simple categorizations.

PRODUCERS TO KNOW

Analemma	Division Winemaking Company
Argyle	Johan Vineyards
Art + Science	Mellen Meyer
Brooks	Soter Vineyards
Day Wines	Swick Wines

The Wine List

Brooks Extended Tirage Sparkling Riesling ($$)

From Oregon's most storied riesling specialist comes this traditional-method version that nods to German Sekt by way of the Willamette Valley: dry, fresh, citrusy, and not at all shy when it comes to doling out its tongue-cleansing acidity.

Analemma "Atavus" Blanc de Noirs ($$)

Repping Oregon's bubbly new wave, Analemma's single-vineyard, vintage-dated pinot noir–based sparkler comes from some of the oldest vines in the Columbia Gorge. In the glass, it pours a copper onion-skin color, just a hue shy of rosé, and delivers an opulent mouthful of tangerine peel and ginger-like spice.

Day Wines "Mamacita!" Pétillant-Naturel ($)

As Oregon's younger generation continues to push the boundaries and reinvent the rules, the results rarely get more exciting than Brianne Day's eclectic lineup of wines. A heady blend of vermentino, muscat, and malvasia, her "Mamacita!" pét-nat is unexpected in all the right ways, proving that there's life in the state beyond pinot noir.

Division Winemaking Company "Gamine" Grenache Pétillant ($$)

Along with her business partner Thomas Monroe, urban winemaker Kate Norris has been making some of the state's definitive natural wines since 2010, but she more recently began releasing her own line under the name "Gamine." This peachy, herb-tinged grenache from the Mae's Vineyard in the Applegate Valley conjures the south of France by way of Portland.

The Northeast
New York and Vermont

If New York state doesn't immediately spring to mind as a major player in the domestic wine game, that's partly because its main growing regions—the Finger Lakes and Long Island—came of age so late. Today, however, New York—as well as its emerging northeastern peer, Vermont—has arrived at a pivotal moment. As it prepares to break out of local markets to become a national contender, the state is becoming known as a source of cool-climate wines that fully embrace their East Coast origins. And as luck would have it, part of that evolution necessarily involves bubbles.

Between Long Island and the Finger Lakes, the latter has arguably come the furthest—in terms both of quality and of carving out a clear identity. The region officially entered its modern era in the 1960s and 1970s, when two visionary immigrants—Dr. Konstantin Frank, a Ukrainian-born scientist with a doctorate in viticulture, and Hermann J. Wiemer, a native of Germany's Mosel region—arrived in the area, positioning the Finger Lakes as North America's answer to the storied wines of Germany, with riesling as its centerpiece.

Both of their wineries turn out several traditional-method sparklers using classic grapes such as chardonnay and pinot noir as well as such Teutonic specimens as riesling. A regional touchstone, Dr. Konstantin Frank's "Sparkling Riesling Nature," for instance, pays homage to German Sekt by way of the area's Keuka Lake terroir. A glimpse of the area's cutting-edge can be found at the biodynamically farmed Bloomer Creek winery, which puts out several riesling-based pét-nats, including a skin-fermented (that is, orange wine) version that tastes like dried apricots and honey.

Though less established, Long Island has also made significant head-way in recent years as a kind of East Coast analogue to France's Loire Valley. Cabernet franc–based reds have emerged as a strong suit, but plenty of intriguing sparkling wines are to be found as well, particularly in the pét-nat arena.

Christopher Tracy's Channing Daughters winery, located in the town of Bridgehampton, now functions as a creative laboratory dedicated to uncovering the great unknown that is Long Island's terroir, including at least ten different ancestral-method wines from grapes both familiar (merlot, cabernet sauvignon) and strange (lagrein, tocai friulano, and muscat ottonel, among others). A similar spirit reigns at the North Fork's Macari Vineyards, which, for one of the island's larger producers, has managed to rack up significant street cred as a pioneer of organic and biodynamic farming. Based on cabernet franc, its "Horses" pét-nat is chock-full of strawberries with an echo of green bell pepper that is the grape's hallmark.

PRODUCERS TO KNOW

Bloomer Creek Vineyards	Dr. Konstantin Frank Winery
Channing Daughters	Macari Vineyards

High on Hybrids: The Next Chapter of American Sparkling Wine

From the fauns and satyrs of ancient Greece to the modern-day labradoodle, humanity's fascination with hybrid creatures spans the ages. As a principle, what's not to like? You take the most compelling aspects of two (or more) disparate things and combine them into something new. Realistically, though, the results don't always turn out as one might wish. Just ask the guy who created the spork.

For better or for worse, that's how we've long considered the hybrid wine grape. As a family, hybrids are born out of crossing the European *Vitis vinifera* vine species (the one responsible for giving us pinot noir, chardonnay, and pretty much every other grape we know by name) with the wild-growing North American *V. labrusca* and *V. riparia*. These ampelographic underdogs were initially bred more for their disease resistance and ability to withstand extreme cold than for their quality. So while they can survive the frigid winters of Vermont or Ohio, conventional wisdom has historically written them off as vitis non grata when it comes to making great wine.

Given the tendency of certain hybrids to exhibit the intensely floral, musky flavors known as "foxiness" (think Welch's grape jelly, but not in a good way), France and Italy have banned hybrids from classified wine production for decades. In America, early examples such as Cayuga, Concord, and Catawba enjoyed a brief heyday during the first decades of the twentieth century, fueling local wine industries across the Northeast and Midwest. But then came Prohibition, and by the time we woke up from the collective stupor, our hopes had already turned toward California, a place far more compatible with the nation's newfound "fine wine" ambitions.

If you had predicted a decade ago that hybrid wines would not only be considered cool but also eventually come to represent one of the most exciting movements in American wine, nobody would have believed you. And yet that is exactly where we are today. From New York's Finger Lakes and Hudson Valley regions to Vermont, Maryland, and even Maine, a small but growing band of winemakers has embraced hybrids with the respect traditionally reserved for vinifera grapes. In the process, they're adding a whole new frontier to the US wine scene that pulls from every page of the postmodern playbook.

Skin-contact whites? Check. Chuggable reds? You bet. However, the most emblematic expression of this current radicalism has been an outpouring of diverse sparkling wines. From takes on the Champagne method and crown-capped pét-nats to cans of gently fizzy piquette and even cider-like coferments with fruit (for example, apples and cranberries), the movement has become a breeding ground for some of the country's most experimental sparkling wines.

The fact that practically everyone operating under the hybrid umbrella has gravitated toward sparkling should come as no surprise. By necessity, cold-hardy hybrids tend to be planted in parts of the country where vinifera grapes struggle to survive. As cold-climate grapes, they're capable of ripening to peak maturity while retaining the bracing acidity that naturally lends itself to bubbles. To wine drinkers raised on European grapes (in other words, all of us), the results can be puzzling. Their flavors and aromas skew in unexpected directions, highlighting intense, sometimes exaggerated fruit (pineapples, lemon curd, strawberries), but rarely exhibit the richness and high alcohol we associate with those same ripe qualities in vinifera-based wines.

According to master sommelier Pascaline Lepeltier and winemaker Nathan Kendall, who produce two hybrid-based pét-nats under their Finger Lakes–based chëpìka label, there was never any doubt that sparkling wine would be their main emphasis. Their decision to focus on hybrids—in this case, the Delaware and Catawba varieties—came as the logical extension of their naturalist philosophy. In cold, wet regions such as the Finger Lakes, growing the *vinifera* species organically presents serious challenges; hybrids, on the other hand, can thrive without pesticides or chemical sprays. After researching the history of those grapes in the region and discovering that sparkling hybrids from the Finger Lakes enjoyed widespread acclaim during the nineteenth century, the rest of the concept quickly fell into place.

Fermented with natural yeasts and bottled without the addition of sulfur, chëpìka's low-alcohol sparklers perfectly align with the current state of the art. As a rediscovery of the region's roots, what Lepeltier and

Kendall are doing isn't all that dissimilar from the work that progressive winemakers are doing in so many other parts of the world to uncover lost styles and expressions under the banner of natural wine. But for those working with newer hybrids in less established areas of the country, there isn't any history—forgotten or otherwise—to draw upon for guidance.

The first signs of Vermont's unlikely ascendency as an experimental hotbed for hybrid winemaking came courtesy of winemaker Deirdre Heekin's La Garagista winery, one of the category's early pioneers and guiding lights of natural wine. From the start, ancestral-method sparklers formed the core of the project. Today, she makes several galvanizing pét-nats, including three under the "Ci Confonde" label (a white, red, and rosé from hybrids such as brianna, Frontenac gris, and Marquette). In addition to proving that hybrid grapes could make compelling, site-specific wines, they've served as the inspiration for others, such as Ethan Joseph, winemaker at Vermont's Shelburne Vineyard. Several of the hybrids he grows for his own Iapetus project, such as the red-skinned Marquette and the white La Crescent, introduced by the University of Minnesota in the early 2000s, have existed for fewer than two decades. From these grapes and others, like l'acadie blanc, he produces a vibrant lineup of pét-nats, though he experiments with other styles as well.

Working from scratch without recourse to any established precedent or data points is no easy task. It requires a specific sort of mind-set: the willingness to be guided by instinct and intuition rather than by-the-numbers predictability. Just ask Todd Cavallo and Crystal Cornish of Wild Arc Farm, who left Brooklyn in 2016 with virtually no enological training to pursue a dream of crafting natural wine and cider in the Hudson Valley. Now in its fourth year, Wild Arc's fizzy offerings run the stylistic gamut. Along with a traditional-method blend of riesling and traminette (a hybrid descended from gewürztraminer) that is refermented with local wildflower honey and fashioned after German Sekt, they also make a handful of standout pét-nats, including their "Checking All the Boxes," a strawberryish blend of Marquette and traminette from the Amorici Vineyard in Washington County, New York.

Proof of just how experimental the US Northeast scene has become, several of its most fearless practitioners aren't even limiting themselves to the use of grapes. For example, Wild Arc's "Sweetheart" bottling, which bills itself as an "Apple + Grape Sparkling Wine," is made by aging Northern Spy apple juice on teroldego grape skins, then adding wildflower honey to jump-start the secondary fermentation in bottle.

Is it wine? Is it cider? Or something else entirely? These existential questions don't trouble the small but growing group of producers, including Vermont's La Garagista and Fable Farm Fermentory, among others, who have started to create hybrid creatures of a different sort. By cofermenting wine grapes (sometimes vinifera, sometimes hybrids) with other fruits, such as apples and pears, they're testing the boundaries of what sparkling wine can be. And why not? The northeastern states were churning out cider centuries before anyone dreamed of growing wine grapes there.

The genre-bending offspring of this unlikely mash-up reveal a whole new perspective on the question of terroir. Consider, for instance, La Garagista's whimsically titled "Stolen Roses," an homage to pomada, a bygone style of northern Italian cider made by fermenting fresh cider on grape skins in large wooden vats. Transporting this tradition to the alpine climate of Vermont, the winery uses Marquette or Frontenac noir grapes and cider from a mix of wild and cultivated apples that grow on the property. No matter what you call it, it's the rare sort of hybrid that unequivocally works.

PRODUCERS TO KNOW

chëpika	Oyster River Winegrowers
Iapetus	Wild Arc Farm
La Garagista Farm + Winery	

The Wine List

Channing Daughters "Rosso" Pétillant-Naturel ($)

It's hard to keep track of how many pét-nats Christopher Tracy now makes over at Channing Daughters. His "Rosso," a kitchen-sink blend of merlot, syrah, cabernet franc, blaufränkisch, and the rare northern Italian refosco, drinks a lot like a bottle-fermented Lambrusco, with an iodine quality that is the calling card of Long Island's clay soils.

La Garagista Farm + Winery "Ci Confonde" Sparkling Rosé ($$)

"Ci Confonde" translates as "confounds us," but there's nothing surprising about how quickly La Garagista's ancestral-method wines have become staples of the American natural-wine scene. Based on the University of Minnesota hybrid Frontenac gris, it's full of rose hips, pomegranate, and moist earth, bringing to mind certain bright, transparent reds (for instance, schiava) from the Italian Alps.

chëpika Catawba Pét-Nat ($)

According to winemaker Nathan Kendall, the Catawba grape, given its ability to preserve acidity even at extreme levels of ripeness, is perfect for sparkling wine. Fermented with ambient yeast, unsulfured, and aged six months in bottle before disgorgement, chëpika's rosé-like take on the grape possesses a rhubarb sourness that lends an edge to its wild-berry fruit.

Iapetus "Figure 1" Pétillant-Naturel ($)

Part of the reason the ancestral method takes so kindly to hybrids, like l'acadie blanc (the variety in question here), is the way the fermentation in bottle adds a savory depth and complexity to the grape's extroverted fruit. Imagine a lightning bolt of pineapple and candied lemon striking through a cloud of yeast.

Pairing Sparkling Wine with Food

Despite the false logic that has long prevented sparkling wine from claiming its rightful place at the table, bubbles might just be the greatest "food wines" of all, capable of performing where so many of their still brethren fall short. Although the possibilities are endless, here are a few particularly successful outside-the-box pairings that drive home the point.

Pairing: Brut Champagne with tempura.

Why it works: Fried food loves Champagne. That goes double for a plate of crispy, salty tempura, as the wine shares many of the same umami elements found in tentsuyu, the dish's traditional dipping sauce. If possible, opt for a more delicate blanc de blancs with shrimp or seafood; blanc de noirs will be perfect with chicken and meats.

Pairing: Cava rosé with burgers.

Why it works: We're repeatedly told to pair red wine with red meat, but when it comes to a burger, think again. Fleshier than most of its French counterparts, pink Cava brings enough tannin to hold up to the beef and the right balance of fruit and acidity to handle all the fixings (ketchup, pickles, mustard, you name it) that often clash with still reds. As an added bonus, fries always go better with fizz.

Pairing: Bottle-fermented Lambrusco with pepperoni pizza.

Why it works: Lambrusco's ancestral homeland of Emilia-Romagna is widely regarded as the gastronomic capital of Italy. Tailor-made for hearty red-sauce fare, Lambrusco is the quintessential pizza wine. There's just something about that crazy combo of gooey cheese, acidic tomato sauce, and cured meat that calls for a bright, fizzy red.

Pairing: Col fondo Prosecco with macaroni and cheese.

Why it works: Whether it be mac and cheese or tagliolini au gratin, when noodles meet dairy fat you need something cleansing to rinse it all down. Drinkers in the land of Prosecco have been doing exactly that with their glorious carb-heavy cuisine since time immemorial. All the better if it's an unfiltered col fondo example. *Lees-y* and *cheesy* rhyme for a reason.

Pairing: Pét-nat with larb gai (Thai chicken salad).

Why it works: What other wine style could hold its own against the funk of fermented fish sauce, the sweetness of sugar, the heat of red chiles, and the tang of fresh lime? Even better than a cold lager, lo-fi pét-nat checks off all the boxes, especially if you find one with a just a hint of residual sweetness to tame the spice.

Pairing: Bugey-Cerdon with baby back ribs.

Why it works: Sticky, savory, smoky, and sugary—the flavors of barbecue don't easily lend themselves to wine, unless that wine is a slightly off-dry, deep pink Bugey-Cerdon. The fizz makes quick work of the fat, and the wine's subtle sweetness plays nice with the smoke and the spice, hitting the spot just like an ice-cold cola.

Pairing: Moscato d'Asti with Belgian waffles.

Why it works: With its low alcohol and sugar-kissed hint of citrus, Moscato d'Asti is the quintessential breakfast wine—especially if that breakfast involves waffles slathered in strawberries, syrup, and (preferably) whipped cream.

By the Top

crown cap

cork & cage

can

New Frontiers in Sparkling Wine

A WORLD TOUR IN NINE BOTTLES

Having traversed the major stations of today's ever-evolving sparkling wine world map, we arrive at the category's unique postmodern predicament. By reconsidering bubbles as just another expression of place, we're left with a seemingly infinite number of places to be expressed. The category, in other words, no longer fits into one uniform bubble (sorry, couldn't resist).

Considering this diversity, one wonders if it is even possible to speak of sparkling wine as a unified genre. It has become as expansive as the wider world of wine itself—a heterogeneous mashup of techniques and traditions and regional iterations.

As that evolution unfolds, new fizzy frontiers keep popping up so quickly that it's impossible to keep track. So in lieu of a region-by-region breakdown, the best way to delineate where sparkling wine is headed is to focus on some of the specific examples that are pushing the category forward in places not traditionally associated with the style.

For one, the indomitable force that is pét-nat shows no signs of relenting. Truly a borderless movement, its democratizing effect continues to spread far and wide, making bubbles viable without the usual overhead investment in time, labor, and high-tech equipment that previously barred entry to aspiring producers. As the style continues to conquer the globe, places as far-flung as Greece, Mexico, and Nova Scotia have entered the fold, proving that bubbles now know no geographical limitations.

That extends even to the most unlikely of places. Having shaken off decades of Soviet era mediocrity, eastern Europe is quickly becoming a prime fizzy contender—whether through the revival of Hungarian pezsgő, the country's traditional Champagne-method wine that once flowed freely throughout the Austro-Hungarian Empire, or the latest surge of ancestral-method wines popping up in the Czech Republic's Moravia region.

Then there's the entire Southern Hemisphere, where it's not so much a question of whether to make sparkling wine but rather what kind of sparkling wine to make. In addition to dabbling with the ancestral method, like pretty much everywhere else, progressive producers in New Zealand have channeled the cold-climate marginality of their growing areas into traditional-method wines that drink like opposite-pole analogues to Champagne or Franciacorta.

Meanwhile, Australia's booming natural-wine scene has given birth to its own uprising of experimental bubbly, and Chile's revival of extremely old-vine pipeño—the country's traditional farmer's wine reimagined as the latest natural-wine darling—has engendered a handful of sparkling versions from some of the oldest vineyards on the planet. Even South Africa is getting in on the action. Each of the following nine bottles is relevant in its own right. Together, they offer a snapshot of just how broad, eclectic, and unclassifiable the world of sparkling wine has already become.

Domaine Glivanos "Paleokerisio" ($)

Wine has been a fact of life in Greece since the age of Homer, so it might seem ironic to label Greek wine as a "discovery." But that's exactly what Greek wine represents today. From its northern border down to its scenic islands, the country's winemakers are rediscovering their terroirs through the unique prism of native grapes, giving Stateside audiences the chance to discover Greece's ancient wine regions for the first time.

Among the most intriguing emblems of that renaissance is Domaine Glivanos's "Paleokerisio," a slightly off-dry semi-sparkling wine from the mountains of Zitsa in the northwestern region of Epirus. A modern homage to the traditionally oxidative, semisweet fizz of the area's past, it's based off the local debina (a white grape of Balkan origin also found in Albania) and vlahiko (the local signature red) varieties. The process of fermenting the grape juice in contact with the skins gives this low-alcohol amber-hued orange wine a slightly grippy texture and a cider-like funk. The result? A sleeper sommelier sensation that doubles as one of the market's most unexpected crowd-friendly sparklers.

Bichi Winery "Pet Mex" ($)

To most drinkers, it's a surprise that such a thing as Mexican wine even exists. That's exactly what Noel Téllez of the cult Bichi Winery is working to change. Based in the craggy mountains of Baja California, near the village of Tecate just over the Californian border, Téllez founded Bichi in 2014 with the mission of bringing organic farming and raw, low-intervention winemaking (*bichi* means "naked" in a Sonoran dialect) to the area's centuries-old heritage vineyards.

Running the winery solo since 2017, Téllez has solidified Bichi's reputation as an essential addition to Latin America's burgeoning lo-fi wine scene. Though he produces several different wines from both his own biodynamic vineyards and in collaboration with a number of organic farmers in the Valle de Guadalupe, his "Pet Mex" pét-nat rosé was the first to achieve breakout success. Sourced from a single parcel of high-elevation vines planted 1,066 feet above sea level to a grape variety that remains unidentified to this day, it's the strawberry-scented, gently fizzy ambassador of a new era in Mexican wine.

Milan Nestarec "Danger 380 Volts" Pét-Nat ($)

Even five years ago, no one would have pegged the Czech Republic as a potential hot zone for new-wave winemaking. That unlikely transformation is due almost entirely to a small group of winemakers based in Moravia, the country's main growing region, who have gathered under the banner of the Autentisté (Authenticists) movement to advocate old-fashioned methods and a return to terroir.

One of the movement's most vocal leaders, Milan Nestarec has emerged as the enfant terrible of central Europe's naturalist fringe. Despite their irreverent names (such as "WTF," "Royale with Cheese," and "GinTonic"), Nestarec's creations number among the Czech Republic's most inventive wines. A mix of three white grapes of vaguely Austro-Hungarian ancestry—Müller-Thurgau, neubürger, and muscat— his "Danger 380 Volts" pétillant-naturel is as joyously drinkable as any in the market. With its citrusy jolt of acidity, it's also more than deserving of its name.

Mother Rock "Force Celeste, Cuvée PN" ($)

Ever since 1992, when the ban on the term *Champagne method* forced South Africa's sparkling wine industry to come up with a term of its own, the country's bubbly ambitions have revolved around Méthode Cap Classique (MCC), produced in the traditional method using the classic Champagne grapes. While those efforts have struggled to stand out from the crowd, a handful of boutique producers have more recently set out to rewrite the narrative about South African fizz.

That includes upstart MCC producers such as Black Elephant Vintners, based in the Franschhoek Valley. But much of the hype surrounding South Africa has centered upon the up-and-coming Swartland area, where a young and naturally minded contingent is flipping the script through a focus on abandoned old vines, a bounty of lesser-known grapes, and a stripped-down aesthetic designed to let those raw materials shine through. To Johan Meyer and Ben Henshaw of Mother Rock Wines, poster children of this iconoclastic new wave, bubbles symbolize just one medium among many for interpreting the area's terroirs. A single-vineyard blend of pinotage (one of South Africa's signature red grapes) and colombard (a white historically used in brandy production), their "Force Celeste, Cuvée PN" reveals their skill with the ancestral method, with its sour-candy tartness and flavors of pink lemonade and guava.

Cambridge Road Pétillant-Naturel "Naturalist" ($)

New Zealand burst onto the international wine scene in the 1990s by hitching its fortunes to an instantly recognizable style of sauvignon blanc from the area of Marlborough. Fresh, screw capped, and unapologetically fruity, these Kiwi expressions have come to define that grape for millions of drinkers, claiming a permanent place on supermarket shelves across the United States in the form of large commercial brands such as Kim Crawford and Cloudy Bay.

But that's hardly the extent of New Zealand's powers. For one, the country is quickly making a name for itself as a wellspring of racy pinot noirs, which has inevitably translated into some of the Southern Hemisphere's most elegant Champagne-method examples. In the meantime, you'll also find such bubblies as this organically farmed, additive-free pét-nat from natural-wine pioneer Cambridge Road. A blend of riesling and pinot gris (along with a bit of chardonnay, pinot noir, and pinot meunier), all sourced from the estate's vineyard in the Martinborough area on New Zealand's North Island, it's about as far removed from the country's mainstream as possible. Briefly fermented in contact with the grape skins, the result isn't quite white or rosé but rather an unclassifiable sparkler that occupies the ambiguous territory in between. In the glass, it's full of juicy apricot and a silty, salty element that evokes its coastal terroir.

Southold Farm + Cellar Piquette ($)

Regan and Carey Meador originally launched Southold Farm + Cellar on the North Fork of Long Island, where they crafted some of New York's most forward-thinking wines. But after a dispute with local officials forced them to shut down, the couple took what, at the time, seemed like an even more radical step: relocating to Gillespie County in the heart of Texas Hill Country. In retrospect, the decision makes perfect sense. As a viticultural blank slate, the Texas hills offered the same creative license that first lured the couple to New York raised to an exponential power.

What greater testament could there be to the project's experimental spirit than its influential role in the American revival of piquette, the low-alcohol, gently effervescent French farmers' wine of eras past. Historically enjoyed as a lunchtime tipple in between backbreaking work in the vines, it's produced by adding water to leftover grape pomace (the stems and skins remaining after pressing) and allowing the mixture to ferment. Offered in a sixteen-ounce can and clocking in at just 4 percent alcohol, Southold's version drinks like some sort of love child between sour beer and rosé: tart and crushable with just a touch of the barnyard to it.

Cacique Maravilla Chacolí Pét-Nat Rosé ($)

After decades of striving to emulate French tradition with Gallic grapes such as cabernet sauvignon and pinot noir, Chile is finally introducing the world to what's truly "Chilean" about Chilean wine. At the heart of that story is the revival of pipeño, the country's traditional light-bodied farmers' wine produced from centuries-old plantings of the humble país grape (known as mission grape in California). Though the style has been produced in the Bio-Bio and Itata regions of Chile's southern Maule Valley since the days of the Spanish missionaries, a new generation has repurposed this local expression for a global audience, tapping into the current fashion for refreshing, minimally processed reds.

As the pipeño revival gains momentum, riding a ripple of attention from boutique US importers specializing in natural wine, the movement's leaders have started to explore other styles as well—notably, pét-nat. Essentially an ancestral-method version of pipeño, this pink-hued example from Cacique Maravilla's Manuel Moraga Gutiérrez in the Bio-Bio Valley, deliberately winks at the in-your-face freshness of Basque txakoli (see page 100). Keep an eye out for Cacique Maravilla's "Gutiflower" as well, a floral, honeyed sparkling wine composed mostly of the muscatel d'Alexandria grape.

Jauma Chenin Blanc Pét-Nat "Blewitt Springs" ($$)

At least to US audiences, Australian wine's public image conformed to two different but equally unfortunate archetypes. At the higher end of the market, an inky, massively ripe style of shiraz (the Aussie name for syrah) rose to the top of wine's pop charts in the 1990s (before just as quickly going bust). And then, of course, who could forget a certain ubiquitous cartoon kangaroo stamped on millions of bottles of the country's leading export? Recently, however, the contours of an alternative Australia—which some have dubbed the New Australia movement—have started coming into focus.

Evidence of this sea change has surfaced across the continent. But the sharpest edge of the New Australian avant-garde can be found in the Adelaide Hills, a cooler growing area just an hour's drive outside the city of Adelaide. It was here that a small band of renegades—notably including James Erksine of the Jauma winery—fomented a naturalist revolution that has disrupted the narrative about Australia. This energy manifests across styles, but one highlight has been an outburst of progressive pét-nats, of which Erksine's "Blewitt Springs" was an early forerunner. Made from old chenin blanc vines, it's complex and savory, reminiscent of lemon pith and scrubby herbs.

Királyudvar Pezsgő "Henye" ($)

In 1730, more than a century before the famous 1855 classification of Bordeaux, Hungary's Tokaj-Hegyalja area became the world's first wine region to establish its own vineyard classification system, which should tell you all you need to know about the sophistication of Hungary's culture. Given this impressive history, Tokaj quickly became a magnet for private investors after the fall of the Iron Curtain, including Anthony Hwang, owner of Vouvray's iconic Domaine Huet estate.

It's not difficult to imagine what motivated Hwang to purchase the celebrated Királyudvar estate in the heart of Tokaj. The area's main grape, furmint, displays the same synthesis of waxy richness, razor-like acidity, and smoky minerality that brings to mind Loire chenin blanc, and it's capable of assuming the same range of styles, from dry to sweet and, of course, sparkling—or, as the Hungarians call it, pezsgő. Inspired by Huet's iconic traditional-method "Pétillant," this biodynamically farmed effort from Királyudvar first appeared in 2007 and offers a similar waxy, honeyed character cut through with a cleansing wash of fizz.

How to Serve Sparkling Wine Like a Pro

Serving Temperature

The myth that sparkling wine should always be served ice-cold (see page 15) still lingers. To the contrary, overly chilling a wine will mute its underlying flavors and aromas. While that might be desirable when it comes to cheap, industrially made sparkling wines, the whole point of drinking honest, terroir-expressive bubbly is to actually taste it.

That said, there's no ideal temperature for all your bubbly needs. In general, because of their richer textures and savory aromas, Champagne and other traditional-method bubblies, including Cava, Franciacorta, and French crémant, show their best with just a slight chill. Think just below room temperature (or room temperature if the room in question happens to be a basement cellar on a rainy day in Champagne). On the other hand, Prosecco and other more delicate and aromatic sparkling wines that display the brighter, fresher flavors of tank fermentation begin to get a bit flabby as they warm up. Here's where a fuller chill truly does the trick, but even then it's possible to overdo it.

The Do's and Don'ts of Cork Extraction

We've all seen a Champagne cork explode across a crowded room. Yes, it sets a celebratory tone but only at the risk of injury to yourself and any innocent bystanders. Here's how to remove that cork like a pro. First, make sure you're working with a properly chilled bottle. If it is too warm, the carbonation will be more aggressive and prone to eruption. Carefully unwrap the foil to expose the cork and the wire cage the French call a muselet. Next, remove that wire muzzle using six twists (fun fact: it's always six), keeping your thumb firmly on top of the cork to prevent any accidental artillery fire. Finally, pointing the bottle away from your face (can't stress this point enough), gently rotate the base of the bottle with one hand while you ever so slowly twist the cork in the opposite direction with the other.

If all goes according to plan, in place of the usual loud "pop!" you'll hear the faintest whisper of gas escaping from the bottle. Of course, you could always make like a Napoleonic soldier and saber off

the neck of the bottle with a sword (or in modern times, a giant butcher's knife), but this approach is generally not recommended for beginners.

The Skinny on Stemware

First, don't overthink your stemware situation. There's no such thing as the perfect sparkling-wine glass, so no need to go out and buy a bunch of fancy new crystal chalices. Whatever you're already using at home for still wines will work just fine. That said, the specific glass shape will impact your experience of drinking the wine. Some folks still prefer the customary flute, which accentuates the carbonation and prevents the bubbles from dissipating too quickly, but many industry pros insist on using a standard white-wine glass because its wider bowl makes it easier to pick out underlying flavors and aromas. Why not try the same wine in multiple glass types to see how each changes the overall impression?

Appendix I
Where to Buy Sparkling Wine

Most, if not all, of the bottles recommended in this book come from independent and family-run producers who make their wines on a human scale. It is only natural, then, that the best places to track them down will be boutique retailers specializing in small-scale, artisanal wines. Following are a handful of the country's top shops, many of which take online orders and ship out-of-state.

Arlequin Wine Merchant,
San Francisco, CA

The Austin Wine Merchant,
Austin, TX

Bacchanal Wine,
New Orleans, LA

Chambers Street Wines,
New York, NY

Crush Wine & Spirits,
New York, NY

Diversey Wine,
Chicago, IL

Division Wines,
Portland, OR

Domaine LA,
Los Angeles, CA

Domestique Wine,
Washington, DC

Flatiron Wine & Spirits,
San Francisco, CA,
and New York, NY

Henry & Son,
Minneapolis, MN

Kermit Lynch Wine Merchant,
Berkeley, CA

K&L Wine Merchants,
Hollywood, Redwood City,
and San Francisco, CA

Leon & Son,
Brooklyn, NY, and
Grand Rapids, MI

Lou Wine Shop,
Los Angeles, CA

Ordinaire Wine Shop & Wine Bar,
Oakland, CA

Perman Wine Selections,
Chicago, IL

Tinys Bottle Shop,
Philadelphia, PA

Vine Wine,
Brooklyn, NY

The Wine Bottega,
Boston, MA

The Wine House,
Los Angeles, CA

Appendix II
Importers to Know

The unprecedented array of sparkling wines we're lucky enough to choose from today would not be possible without the intrepid importers and distributors responsible for championing artisan winemakers and bringing their bottles to US shores. Keep an eye out for the following names; their presence on a bottle's back label guarantees you're getting something good.

Avant-Garde Wine & Spirits

Becky Wasserman Selections

Circo Vino

Coeur Wine Company

David Bowler Wine

De Maison Selections

Grand Cru Selections

Jenny & François Selections

José Pastor Selections

Kermit Lynch Wine Merchant

Louis/Dressner Selections

Martine's Wines

MFW Wine Co.

PortoVino

Polaner Selections

The Rare Wine Co.

Rosenthal Wine Merchant

Schatzi Wines

Selection Massale

Selections de la Viña

Skurnik Wines & Spirits

Super Glou

T. Edward Wines & Spirits

Transatlantic Bubbles

Vom Boden

Weygandt-Metzler Importing

Zev Rovine Selections

Appendix III
Sparkling Wine Glossary

Atmospheric pressure: Measured in units called bars, atmospheric pressure refers to the strength of the CO_2 gas inside a bottle of sparkling wine. The higher the number of bars, the stronger the wine's carbonation will be. Most Champagne-method wines come in at six bars of pressure, whereas the softer bubbles in a bottle of pét-nat or Prosecco generally register between three and four.

Autolysis: As a wine spends time in contact with its lees (the deposit of yeast left over after fermentation), a complex chemical reaction occurs known as autolysis, during which the yeast cells break down and release all kinds of flavorful proteins, amino acids, and carbohydrates into the wine. The resulting rich, nutty, brioche-like tastes and smells (what wine nerds call "autolytic character") is a hallmark of Champagne and other traditional-method wines.

Base wine: To make most sparkling wines, you first need to make a still wine known as the base wine, or what the Champenois call "a vin clair." By refermenting that base wine—in tank or in bottle, as the case may be—it is transformed into a sparkling one.

Blanc de blancs: Originally coined in Champagne, where it almost always indicates a 100 percent chardonnay-based wine, *blanc de blancs* has become a universal term for a sparkling wine made exclusively from white grapes.

Blanc de noirs: A sparkling wine made from the clear juice of red-skinned grapes.

Brut: Indicates a dry sparkling wine. In Champagne, that means fewer than 12 grams of residual sugar per 1 liter of wine.

Crémant: An umbrella term for French bubbly made in the Champagne method from areas outside Champagne (see page 34).

Disgorgement: The process of removing the deposit of dead yeast cells from the neck of a bottle of sparkling wine, or what the French call "dégorgement."

When listed on a wine's back label, the disgorgement date tells you when the wine was bottled (particularly useful information for gauging the age of nonvintage bottles of bubbly).

Dosage: The practice of adding sweetener (sugar or a mix of sugar and wine) to Champagne and other sparklers before bottling to balance the underlying acidity of the wine.

Frizzante: Italian for "softly sparkling," frizzante is the equivalent of French pétillant. Semisweet Moscato d'Asti (see page 82) falls in this category.

Grower: A typically small-scale, independent winemaker who produces sparkling wine from his or her own vineyards. Most commonly associated with the revolutionary movement in Champagne, the term is now widely applied across the globe.

Liqueur de tirage: The solution of wine, yeast, and sugar that is added to the still base wine to cause the secondary fermentation that creates the bubbles in a Champagne-method wine.

Nonvintage: Often abbreviated to NV, this term designates a sparkling wine that consists of a blend of multiple past vintages. Historically, the NV offering would represent a Champagne house's entry-level bottling, but that's increasingly no longer the case today.

Reserve wine: The portion of still wine (or more often, blend of wines) held back from exceptional vintages that is blended with the current vintage to produce a nonvintage sparkling wine.

Spumante: The Italian term for a fully effervescent wine. For reference, Franciacorta (see page 61) is a spumante sparkling wine.

Vintage: A sparkling wine sourced entirely from the fruit of a single year's harvest. Released only when the vintages are outstanding, these wines often represent the top bottlings in a producer's portfolio.

Acknowledgments

Most of this book was written in the midst of the COVID-19 pandemic. Needless to say, the experience of completing a manuscript about sparkling wine—a category historically associated with celebration and the warmth of connection—often felt at odds with our new reality of social distancing and isolation. So first and foremost, thank you to my wife, Adele, for your unconditional love, support, and friendship and for reminding me that it's always the right time for Champagne. This book is dedicated to you.

Thank you to the entire team at Ten Speed Press, but especially to my brilliant editor, Ashley Pierce, for bringing this book to life, and for all your guidance, patience, and insight along the way. Thanks also to Annie Marino, for your invaluable work behind the scenes, and to Nick Hensley, for gracing these pages with such incredible illustrations.

To Talia Baiocchi, my friend and editor at *PUNCH,* for sticking with me all these years, for perpetually pushing me to dig deeper, and for your special knack for seeing the bigger picture. All writers should be so lucky to rely upon editors like you.

Finally, to my parents, Rich and Jackie, for always believing in me and my writing and for never doubting that this weird hobby of mine would ultimately amount to something. You've been there for me every step of the way.

About the Author

Zachary Sussman is a Brooklyn-based wine writer and the author of *The Essential Wine Book* (Ten Speed Press, 2020). His work has appeared in *Saveur, Wine & Spirits, The World of Fine Wine, Food & Wine,* and *WSJ. Magazine,* among many other publications. He is a regular contributor to *PUNCH* and was formerly named the Louis Roederer Mont Blanc Emerging Wine Writer of the Year.

Index

183

Published in the United States by Ten Speed Press, an
imprint of Random House, a division of Penguin Random
House LLC, New York.
www.tenspeed.com

Ten Speed Press and the Ten Speed Press colophon are
registered trademarks of Penguin Random House LLC.

Library of Congress Cataloging-in-Publication Data is
on file with the publisher.

Hardcover ISBN: 978-1-9848-5679-1
eBook ISBN: 978-1-9848-5680-7

Printed in China

Acquiring editor: Julie Bennett
Project editor: Talia Baiocchi
Production editor: Ashley Pierce
Designer: Annie Marino
Art director: Emma Campion
Production designer: Mari Gill
Production manager: Dan Myers
Copyeditor: Sharon Silva
Proofreader: Hope Clarke
Indexer: Ken DellaPenta
Marketer: Chloe Aryeh
Publicist: David Hawk

10 9 8 7 6 5 4 3 2 1

First Edition